Jack the Ripper

A Novel Exploring the Mind of Jack the Ripper

(The Unsolved Mystery of History's Most Notorious Serial Killer)

Mary Cornwall

Published By **Phil Dawson**

Mary Cornwall

All Rights Reserved

Jack the Ripper: A Novel Exploring the Mind of Jack the Ripper (The Unsolved Mystery of History's Most Notorious Serial Killer)

ISBN 978-1-77485-553-9

No part of this guidebook shall be reproduced in any form without permission in writing from the publisher except in the case of brief quotations embodied in critical articles or reviews.

Legal & Disclaimer

The information contained in this ebook is not designed to replace or take the place of any form of medicine or professional medical advice. The information in this ebook has been provided for educational & entertainment purposes only.

The information contained in this book has been compiled from sources deemed reliable, and it is accurate to the best of the Author's knowledge; however, the Author cannot guarantee its accuracy and validity and cannot be held liable for any errors or omissions. Changes are periodically made to this book. You must consult your doctor or get professional medical advice before using any of the suggested remedies, techniques, or information in this book.

Upon using the information contained in this book, you agree to hold harmless the Author from and against any damages, costs, and expenses, including any legal fees potentially resulting from the application of any of the information provided by this guide. This disclaimer applies to any damages or injury caused by the use and application, whether directly or indirectly, of any advice or information presented, whether for breach of contract, tort, negligence, personal injury, criminal intent, or under any other cause of action.

You agree to accept all risks of using the information presented inside this book. You need to consult a professional medical practitioner in order to ensure you are both able and healthy enough to participate in this program.

Table of contents

Chapter 1: The Whitechapel Murders 1

Chapter 2: The Police Were Confused 31

Chapter 3: The Investigation 61

Chapter 4: The Limelight 71

Chapter 5: Let's See If We Can Form A Visual 76

Chapter 6: Prime Suspects 117

Chapter 7: The Art Of Murder 131

Chapter 8: The Jack The Ripper Complex 146

Chapter 9: Largely Rewarding Rewards Were Provided 166

Chapter 10: There Is No More Clarity On The Subject Than 15 Years Ago 178

Chapter 1: The Whitechapel Murders

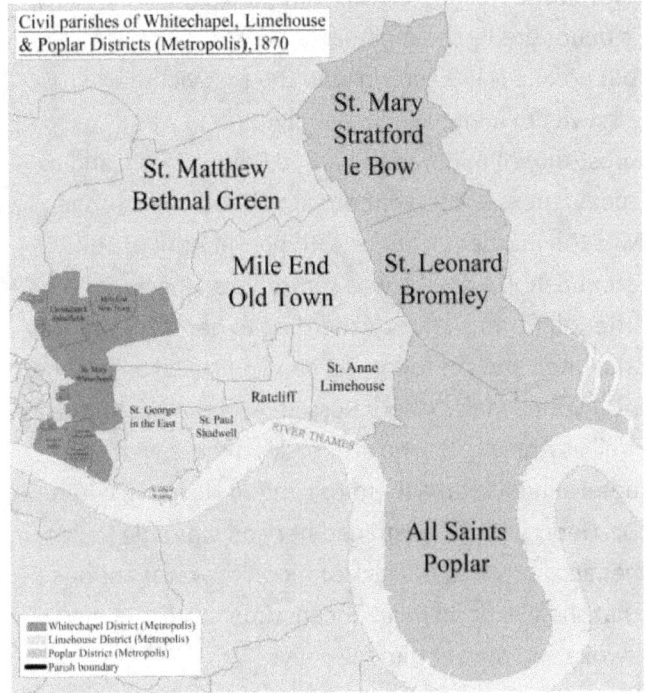

The map shows the Whitechapel district.
"My book is very graphic. I do not apologize for it. However, it's graphic because I spoke the truth regarding what Jack did the Ripper committed to the victims of his crimes." -- Bernard Schaffer, author of

Whitechapel The Last Stand of Sherlock Holmes

Since serial killers are accountable in the murder of a variety of people, it's difficult to figure out who victims are, particularly when authorities don't know who they are searching for. So even though Jack the Ripper is undoubtedly the most famous serial killer of all time but no one is the certain who the first victim was. First victim in the Whitechapel murders was a prostitute of middle age named Emma Smith, and to today, there is a fervent debate about whether she was the murder victim or a Ripper. In April of 1888 around 4:00 a.m. she was spotted walking back home after night-time tricks. According to her story she was assaulted and cut following being of raped and robbed by 4 young males. Mary Russell, who ran the home, as well as Annie Lee, who also resided there were determined to take them to London Hospital, where Dr. George Haslip examined her and was able to hear her account. But, the lack of blood flow was serious that she was soon in an unconscious state and never awoke and died within four days.

Since a tragic ending was not unusual for women working in the East End, the murder was not a huge story in the media However, there were certain questions that needed to be addressed and clarified. Inquests were held to decide the cause of death with the intention that charges could later be filed against the murderer. The problem was that there was nothing for the authorities to base their investigation on, as Smith was unable to identify her attackers and her past was unclear.

Another potential suspect in the murder could be Martha Tabram, who, like Smith was middle-aged, and was a lark for some time following leaving her children and husband. Tabram was discovered early in the morning of the 7th of August in 1888, the day following the Bank Holiday, and witnesses claimed that after she'd been drinking with a prostitute in a nearby bar and then walked with a customer to an alley that connected Wentworth Street and Whitechapel High Street at around midnight. After a few hours her body was discovered with many stab wounds throughout the throat lung, lungs, heart stomach, liver, spleen and the genitals.

Many people who research the Ripper case don't believe that Tabram was one of the Jack the Ripper's as the method of operation differed from the one associated with the other five victims that were slashed in a specific manner which was different from the method in which Tabram was cut. However it is reasonable to speculate that the Ripper's methods changed following his initial victims to a more precise M.O. for his later victims, and one of the primary investigation's investigators, Walter Dew, believed that both Smith as well as Tabram had been victims of the Jack the Ripper.

Martha Tabram's body

Of all the victims who were murdered during this time in the history of London, five have been confirmed by all credible sources to have been murdered by the notorious Ripper and the first victim is Mary Ann Nicholls, who was murdered in the early evening of August 31, which was just days after Tabrum. The injuries Nicholls received were distinct enough from the two previous Whitechapel murders to make distinct distinctions. In addition, the coroner blade is through Ripper Ripper did not result in an excessive amount of blood; Llewellyn noted the blood on the scene was "about adequate to fill up two wine glasses or half one pint at most." The absence of blood caused people to believe that she wasn't killed at the location her body was discovered however, the congealed mass of blood that was found beneath her body suggested that she was murdered in the area and the mutilation likely to be the name of Jack the Ripper's call card was also carried out there.

Buck's Row, where Nicholls was killed.

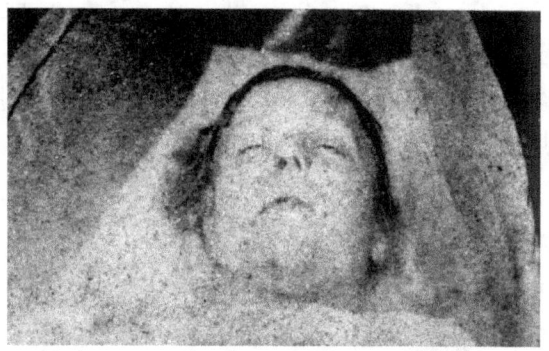

Nicholls" body is ready to be buried

Like a steam engine moving uphill, The Ripper's baffling work increased in speed when August turned into September. On the morning of September 8, less than one day after Nicholls was discovered dead, a second body was discovered.

A 20-year-old James Kent described the ghastly discovery in the following inquest by stating, "James Green and I were together at 29, Hanbury-street. As we walked through the passage, sitting on the stairs to the back of the house I saw a woman lying in the yard , between those steps as well as the divide of the backyard and next. Her head was close to the house, but there was no portion of her person is in the walls. The feet were laid out at the rear of the premises. Deceased's clothes were in disarray and her apron was put over her feet. I didn't go down the staircase, however, I walked out and returned when Inspector Chandler had arrived. I could tell this woman had died. There was a handkerchief that was wrapped around her neck, which appeared to be soaked in blood. The hands and face were covered in blood as if she had fought. It appeared that she was lying on her back, and fighting using her hands in order to release herself. Her hands were pointed towards her throat. The legs were spread wide and there were traces of blood on the legs. The entrails protruded, and lay on the body's left. I purchased a piece canvas from the store to cover the body. By this time, a mob was been gathered, and the inspector Chandler was in charge in the backyard."

Photo of Annie Chapman as a young woman

Photograph of Hanbury Street, the yard in which Annie Chapman was found dead

BLIND-MAN'S BUFF.
(As played by the Bobby.)
"TURN ROUND THREE TIMES,
AND CATCH WHOM YOU MAY."

The 22nd of September 1888 issue of Punch with a rant against police for not being able to determine the identity of the perpetrator

Profilers who deal with criminally insane people often notice that they usually increase the severity and scope that they commit until they are caught. Although there was no arrest, Jack the Ripper seems to fit into this pattern. He could also have been motivated by the growing curiosity about the crimes that remain unsolved in the wake of the murders, as on September 27 on September 27, the Central News Agency received a letter from an anonymous author that claimed that he was the serial murderer. The police were notified on September 29th, the letter was written at "The Boss, Central News Office, London, City" and included the following:
"Dear Boss,
"I keep hearing that the police have arrested me, but they aren't fixing me at this point. I've laughed whenever they seem so clever and claim to be on the right path. The humor about Leather Apron gave me real troubles. I'm a whore's girl and I'm going to quit tormenting them until I become buckled. Great job the last one was. I didn't give the lady any time to shout. I don't know how they can catch me right now. I am awestruck by my job and would love to do it all over again. You'll soon hear about me playing my

humorous games. I threw some of the real red stuff inside a bottle of ginger beer during my last job to write on, but it became thick as glue and I'm not able to use it. Red ink is good enough I'm sure ha ha.

The next task I will do I will cut the lady's ears and give it to police officers for fun, wouldn't you. Then, keep this letter in the back until I've completed a little work, and then send the letter in a straight manner. My knife is so lovely and sharp that I'd like to start working as soon as I get the chance. Best of luck.
"Yours truly
"Jack the Ripper" Ripper
"Dont me bother using the trade name.
"PS Didn't have the confidence to publish this before I cleaned every red ink off of my hands. I'm still cursing it. so far. The internet says I'm now a doctor. ha ha"

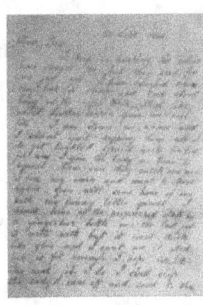

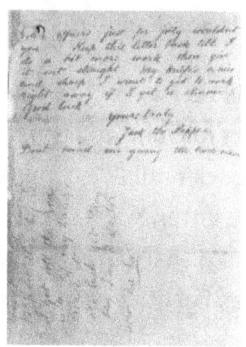

Photos taken from "Dear Boss" letter

Authorities were already accustomed for receiving fraudulent letters sent by pranksters and those who wanted to be in the limelight however they could. Police initially dismissed the case as an untrue story. The speculation regarding"the "Leather Apron" killer was already in the newspapers, and everyone who read the letters was aware of the nickname being tossed around. But, on the night the police received the letter The Jack the Ripper struck in a manner that appeared to confirm an explicit promise he made in his letter, that would not only cause the release of his "Dear Boss" letter, but also lead to the rebranding of the murderer "Jack the Ripper" for the rest of time. In actuality the early the morning of the 30th of September, 1888, brought the most fatal of the crime spree of Jack the Ripper. The first woman to be victim to the killer is Elizabeth Stride, whose body was discovered shortly after midnight in the vicinity of the International Workmen's Club. Doctor. Frederick Blackwell observed, "The victim lay on her side, lying obliquely across the passageway and her face was pointing at the wall to her right. The legs were dangling and her feet were pressed against the wall on the right-hand part of the corridor. Her head was resting on the rut in the carriage-wheel, with the neck resting on the rut. Her feet were just three feet from the entrance. Her dress was loose around her neck. The chest and neck were hot, and the legs. The face was a little warm. Hands were cold. One hand had been opened placed on the chest and covered in blood. The left hand lying on the ground was closed partially and contained a small packet of cachous, wrapped inside tissue. There were no rings, and there were no the marks of rings, or marks of rings, on the hands. The face was quite calm. Its mouth seemed slightly open. The deceased was wearing around her neck was a check silk scarf that had a bow, which was turned left and pulled extremely tight. Inside the neck was an incision that was in line to the lower border that the scarf. The border was a little frayed like an abrasive knife. The neck incision began on the left about 2 inches below the jaw's angle and was almost exactly in line with it, almost cutting the vessels on the left side, and cutting the windpipe into two pieces, before ending on the opposite end 1 centimeter lower than the angle on the jaw on the right however without cutting the vessels on the side. I was unable to determine if the bloody hand had actually been moved. The blood was flowing down the drain to the drain in the opposite direction to the feet. There was around 1 lb of blood clotted near the body and an entire stream from there until the back door of the club."

It's possible the fact that the Ripper didn't finish his M.O. upon Elizabeth Stride made it possible for him to murder another victim a little over an hour afterward. Police were hardly able to cleanse Stride's blood from their hands when they received another report of a different victim. The victim involved Catherine Eddowes.

The policeman Edwards Watkin discovered the body and told the story of the incident: "I next came into Mitre-square around 1.44 When I spotted bodies lying in the left as I came into the square. The woman was lying on her back with her feet toward the square. Her clothes were scattered. I noticed the throat had been cut, and her stomach was ripped open. The body was lying in an area of blood. I did not even touch her body. I walked across the street towards Kearley as well as Long's storage facility. The door was open and I tried to push the door open and I called the watchman Morris who was in the building. Morris came out. I stayed with him until the arrival by Police-constable Holland. There was no one else there prior to that, except myself. Holland was then joined by Dr. Sequeira. Inspector Collard arrived at around 2 hours later, as did the Dr. Brown, surgeon to the police force."

Due to the severe mutilation sustained by the previous victims, it is almost impossible to conviction that the Ripper might be more brutal however there was no evidence that the Whitechapel murders to date had been as horrific as the murder of Eddowes. Doctor. Brown, called upon to once again assess the deceased, gave many information:

"The body was lying on its back, with the head was turned to the left shoulder. The arms were by the side of the body, as were falling into the side of the body. The palms were raised, the fingers bent slightly. A thimble lay on fingers on right. The clothes were pulled up over the stomach. The thighs were not covered. The left leg was extended along the body. It was visible to the abdomen. Right leg bent between the knee and thigh.

"The bonnet was located at to the side of the head, causing a huge disfigurement to the face. The throat was cut. The area below the throat contained the neckerchief. ... The intestines were dragged out to an extensive extent and then placed on top of the right shoulder. They were then smearmed over with a feculent substance. A portion of around two feet was completely detached from the body, and then placed in between body and left arm probably through deliberate design. The auricle and the lobe in the right ear had been cut through. There was a large amount of blood clotted on the road to the left of the neck, around the shoulder and the upper part of the arm. There was also the blood-colored fluid that had flowed from under the neck towards on the shoulder to with the pavement sloped downwards in that direction.

"Body was very warm. No death stiffening was taking place. It is likely that she died probably within the next half an hour. We examined her for superficial bruises but saw no. No blood was seen on the abdomen's skin or any secretion on the legs. There is no blood splatter on the concrete or the floor around. There were no blood marks beneath the center part of the body. There were several buttons in the blood clotted when the body was taken off. No blood was found on the outside of the clothing. There were no signs of any recent connections...

"The face was a lot damaged, including the eyelids, jaw, the nose, the lips, the cheeks and the mouth had cuts. There were scratches under that left ear. A cut was made in the throat to the size of 6 or 7 inches. The reason for death was hemorrhage that occurred in the throat. The death occurred immediately and the mutilations took place following the death ... There was not many blood marks on the murderer. The cut was caused by a person on one side sitting down below the center in the body. ... It was discovered that the uterus had been cut off leaving only a tiny part as well as the kidney on left was removed. Both of these organs were missing and were not located. According to me, the woman was lying on her back. The way the kidney was removed indicated that it was done by someone who was aware of what he was about. It was surely an extremely sharp knife, and at the very least 6 inches. in length... What pieces taken out would not be of any value for any professional use. It took a lot of experience to be able to remove the kidney, and also to determine the location of it. The knowledge may be available to those who are in the habit of cutting animals...I believe that he was able to do it in a reasonable amount of time, however it was likely accomplished quickly. It could be completed in five minutes. It could take longer, but that's the shortest amount of time it can be accomplished in. ... I am certain there was no fight. I have any reason to believe that it was the work of a single man."

Police doctor Thomas Bond claimed the mutilation wasn't particularly exact: "In each case the victim was someone who did not have understanding of anatomical science or research. My opinion is that this man does not even have the technical skills of a butcher, horse slaughterer, or anyone else familiar with cutting dead animal carcasses." But the likeness between the ways Eddowes was mutilated as well as the way Chapman was cut up made clear that both were victimized by the exact same murderer and the fact that a portion of Eddowes right ear been cut off suggested that the person who wrote"Dear Boss," the "Dear Boss" letter was the one who committed the murder.

Bond

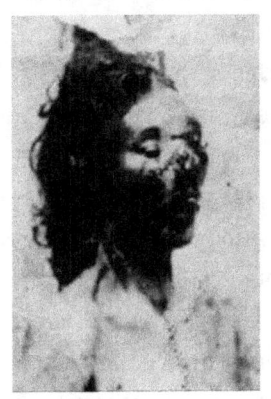

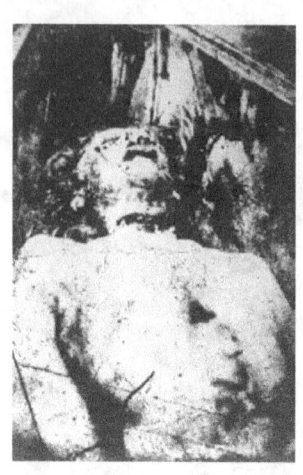

Photos of the postmortem of Eddowes

A controversial pieces of writing likely written by the murderer came just after the murder. "Saucy Jacky" postcard "Saucy Jacky" postcard was delivered on the 1st day of October one day following the double murder. it reads,

"I wasn't codding [sic]my dear old Boss to give you the hint, you'll be hearing about Saucy Jacky's job tomorrow. Double event , this time the first squeezed a bit but didn't get it right away. Didn't have the time to remove his ears for the police to express my thanks for keeping the last letter until I returned to work. Jack the Ripper"

It is believed that the Saucy Jacky postcard was published in a time that was long enough after the facts were made public for any person to have made references to the "double incident," however, it is thought to be real partly due to the emphasis placed on the ears (similar in similar to the "Dear Boss" letter) and the fact that it was signed by Jack the Ripper within a few days of it was sent out in response to the Dear Boss letter and before the name was widely in use.

Because of this, many have been speculating for years that the person who composed the "Dear Boss" letter was also the one who sent the postcard, regardless of whether they actually were the murderers or not. For instance, forty years later, in 1931, the journalist Fred Best of The Star claimed to be the one who wrote the letters that were signed "Jack The Ripper" to "keep the business alive" however, Best isn't the first person to claim years later that he did not want to be a spotlight.

No matter who wrote it the postcard has disappeared from the police file and never returned to the archives.

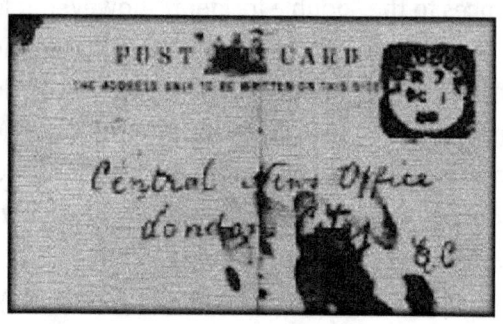

A reproduction from the Saucy Jacky postcard
The next victim of the Ripper and the final one that everyone believes was killed by him is Mary Jane Kelly, who was discovered dead in her bed on the 9th of November. Alongside the possibility that she was killed in her bed, not in the streets There are a lot of other peculiarities that surround Kelly's death. One of them is that at age 25 her age, she was much younger than other victims. Furthermore her body was more badly damaged than any of the victims before her were, possibly because the perpetrator was comfortable enough inside to spend his time.

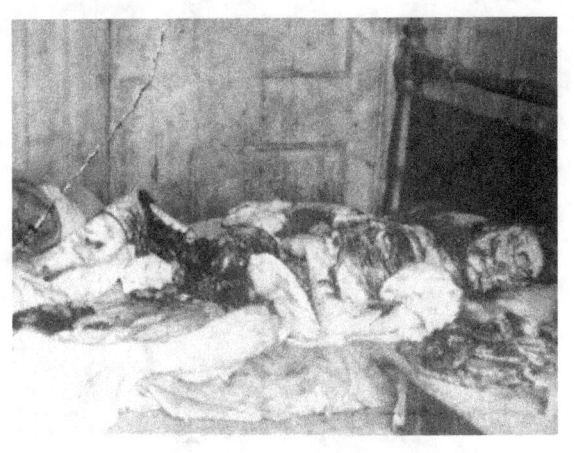

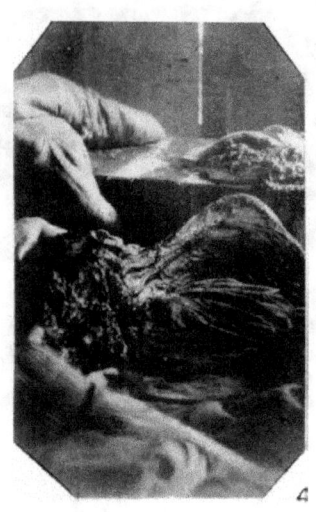

Photos of the body of Mary Kelly

Most people agree there was a consensus that Jack the Ripper killed Nicholls, Chapman, Stride, Eddowes and Kelly and Kelly, but that's not the point at which the consensus ceases. The debate continues over what transpired with Jack the Ripper after the Kelly murder and the theories range from the murderer leaving London and dying or even being imprisoned to murder more people around Whitechapel. It is evident that the murders that took place in the area didn't end until the month of November 1888. Indeed, the murders continued for the next few years.

The woman who passed away within a short time immediately after Kelly died was Rose Mylett, whose body was discovered in the month of December in 1888. The reason why she's not thought to be Ripper-related Ripper victim is a result of geographical location (her body wasn't found in Whitechapel but was found in close by Poplar) however there are a variety of distinctions in her demise and the one of the canonical five.

The authorities initially wondered if she was spared the mutilation because the murderer was in a state of shock before he got the chance to react or was murdered by a different predator entirely. Robbery isn't believed to have been the motive as she was still carrying some money in her pocket however that wouldn't have eliminated a case of pure brutality or passion. Some even went as far to say that although a jury found that it was a murder committed with intent, she died in a natural manner however the suspects were never identified.

In mid-year 1889 the fear in Whitechapel began to diminish at the very least but the concerns were raised after the remains of Alice McKenzie was found in Castle Alley on July 17. In the coroner's inquiry, "Dr. George Baxter Phillips, divisional surgeon for the H Division, said that was summoned, and arrived at

Castle-alley around 1:10 a.m. on Wednesday morning, as it began to rain heavily. ... He described the injuries that were a number, and they were mostly superficial cuts that were located on the lower portion of the body. There were several scars from the past as well as an injury to the upper part of the thumb on the right side, which was caused by an earlier injury. The neck injury was about 4 inches. long and extended through the back of the muscles that were nearly entirely separated. It reached the front part of the neck up to an area of 4 inches. under the chin. The second incision was made below the chin that must have started from behind and was immediately beneath the initial. The reason for death was syncope resulting due to the loss of blood from the split carotid vessels. This death could have been almost immediate."

The issue was evidently, that numerous females and males died by similar methods in the dreadful section of town. Because more than six months had passed since the most recent Ripper incident, as well because there was no sign of dismemberment, McKenzie's demise is usually not thought as part of the work of the thief.

Postmortem image of McKenzie

JACK THE RIPPER.
WHO IS HE? WHAT IS HE?
WHERE IS HE???

A September 21st, 1889 issue of Puck calling out the
police's inability of identifying Jack the Ripper
The area was quiet for a couple of months, before the
subsequent horrific crime was discovered. The second
time, there was no possibility of naming the victim
since only one female torso was discovered in a
hidden archway on Pinchin Street. It is tempting to
believe that it was caused by Jack the Ripper and that
the serial killer would continue murdering - since Jack
the Ripper was not identified, and so we don't have
any reason for believing that he could simply cease
killing following the Kelly murder. However, it is
important to be aware of the others who committed
serial murders in the vicinity. For instance, just a few
weeks after Eddowes and Stride were killed the
headless body from a woman discovered inside the
underground of the newly constructed Metropolitan
Police headquarters in Whitehall. The pattern of
mutilation found in this case was similar to that of the
Parchin Street killing, but police concluded that Jack
the Ripper wasn't responsible for the "Torso killer"
due to the starkly different method of operation.
In reality after six months, another body was
discovered in the the same location, beneath the arch

of a railway. Frances Coles was only about 30 when she was killed. As the other victims, she was also an "fallen female." But apart from the place of her body as well as her job, there's nothing else that can tie them to Ripper victims.

Naturally, it would be a while before people would stop wondering or even admitting for themselves, what each fresh murder that occurred in Whitechapel was a sign of the return of Jack the Ripper and, while it's unclear what (if one or more) among the remaining Whitechapel murders were carried out by the notorious serial killer, the only thing that is certain is that the sequence of murders came to an end in 1892. The police actually had stopped adding evidence and records to the official file of Jack Ripper file in 1896. Ripper files in 1896, at which they had already conducted interviews with several suspects.

Chapter 2: The Police Were Confused

"Several days went by without any clues being discovered. The police were also confused. The media started to condemn and speak about inefficiency. The public then joined in the call for reform. This was a travesty. Police were doing the best they could in human terms. To enhance their own image, apart from their natural need to take revenge for a terrible crime They were determined to win. But there was one thing that our critics did not see. The murder, as was all of the Ripper murders and the other Ripper murders, added a burden placed on a group of men already gruellingly overworked. Others were also being perpetrated and criminals were required to be pursued. The life of a police officer in Whitechapel at the time was a long and arduous nightmare. It's not common to connect to the same individual two murders that took places within months of each other. This is why in this case it wasn't until some moment following Martha Turner had met her fate that the idea was raised it was possible that Emma Smith might have been the first victim of the same killer." The Detective Constable Walter Dew.

Although no pain can be comparable with the suffering of those who were people who were victims of Ripper and their families however, one should be able to feel some sympathy for the officers and investigators charged with locating the devious and vicious killer. In reality, the investigation of the murders fell under the jurisdiction of not two but one police force due to the fact that Scotland Yard was responsible for investigating all crimes across all the Boroughs of London apart from one: London City. City of London itself, with their own police department. In the incident of the Whitechapel murders the police came under scrutinization not just in London but around the world as well, with Americans finding themselves fascinated by the ways the police's organization and practices were distinct from and similar to those of America. United States. On the 16th of October 1888, during the height of the excitement and mania, at the height of the mania, Atchison Daily Globe in Kansas published the following article: "London has been more disturbed because of The Whitechapel murders than any other incident in recent years. The possibility there were so many female victims were able to be killed, clearly in the same way and that the killer for so long escape the London police comes as a shock to the Londoners who believe they have the most effective police force around the globe. But, it's the London detective police force, not officers, whose primary task is to find out those responsible for crimes even though detectives are just a different kind of police. In 1877, the London detective police was organized in 1877, and since then has been considered to be extremely efficient. Prior to this time, the force was comprised of a few detectives per district, under the supervision of the captain or superintendent of the district. The force also consisted of 30 men in the central office in Scotland Yard. The result was that there were various separate détachments."

The article continued to discuss the changes made to the London police force over the last few years to modernize its procedures and bring them to the end of the 19th century. "On April 8th, 1878, an reform took effect The purpose of the reform was to strengthen the police force and also to consolidate the authority that it operated. The control of the force falls into its control by a brand new department, one of criminal investigation. It is under the direction that of Scotland Yard's director. Scotland Yard. In every city division, each city division, there's a local inspector who is in charge of the detectives in his divisionand is supposed to serve as an agent for the director but is actually under the supervision by the director. If the system is complicated or insufficient to be practical for detective work investigations are conducted in a fairly independent manner by divisions, however the notion that Scotland Yard being the center of all investigation work is governed is maintained by the public. Inspectors gather there at times and local superintendents submit report of the crimes that occurred in the past 24 hours each day, and the director has to give instructions to their reports, however, in practice, inspectors are autonomous in the event of any crime will usually be transferred in

their hands."
In addition to providing readers with this background, the article then moved into a detailed description of the department's current organizational structure: "The detective force of London comprises 400 men during summer and 700 during winter. They are selected from the police force for their inventiveness for securing criminals, so in the sense that it is evident. They are the Scotland Yard force consists of 80 men, most of whom are inspectors."

Like modern-day detective dramas 19th Century detective stories are often referred to as "Penny Dreadfuls" were full of inaccurate information regarding how crimes were dealt with particularly with the help of Scotland Yard, another fact the article highlighted. "This agency has often been the center of investigation in the criminal justice system It has been asked repeatedly to help the writer, particularly one who has a plot that covers the subject of a crime, or who writes detective stories that its fame has grown global from just this source and without a thought of the numerous amazing criminal cases it has dealt. Novelists have frequently taken liberties when it comes to Scotland Yard rules. Scotland Yard is a force that operates in London all by itself, with being a London detective is rarely assigned to any other place. But many a storyteller has requested the services of a Scotland Yard detective to help the plot and to travel where the chief wouldn't ever think of sending him. With the novelist, everything is possible. the inspector shows up and, if the nimbleness as a real police officer and the luck of his detective were just a tiny fraction of the story they tell found in the book, no guilty person would ever be able to escape. The police force is under the direct supervision of the deputy commissioner. It is tasked with investigating notable crimes such as Whitechapel murders, for instance. Whitechapel murders, however its primary task is to investigate embezzlements and forgeries as well as similar issues. The force also conducts a good amount of government work as well as for the British crown and governments in other nations. The force is also required to look into every naturalization application and to attend gatherings of the public, as well as keeping an eye on the professional criminals that could be in the wild. Every week, the Scotland Yard detective goes to the prisons in the city to examine the prisoner who are awaiting trial, and check which ones are known to the policeman. Foreign correspondence is a crucial aspect. The work used to be done by a group of civil service officers. The work is now done in Scotland Yard, and each correspondence is answered in the language it was written."One among the most difficult aspect of the Whitechapel murders was the fact that the detectives charged with locating the murderer were unable to determine the exact date the murder took place. Many believed the victim, Emma Smith, who had passed away the day of her death, April 4 which was the day following Easter, could have was his initial victim however others weren't certain. Walter Dew, one of the primary investigators of this case later noted it was not anything in the case that suggested that it was the work of an infamous serial killer.

"The public was not aware of that. The police did not either. What could they have done? The murder itself, except the peculiar kind of injuries was not a new phenomenon in Whitechapel. There are those who doubt the possibility that killing Mrs. Smith was the handiwork of the Ripper. In some ways, the crime differed from subsequent crimes. The woman who was mutilated, however but not subjected to the horrific abuse that was exhibited to the victims who were later mutilated. None of the other bodies was found in such a crowded and well-used thoroughfare like Osborne Street. In dark alleys and shady courts were the locations the monster picked to bring rapid death to the other women who were frightened to fall into his hands. The locations of the murders appeared to have been carefully picked. However, it is important to remember that If it was the first Ripper murder, it was not the first. The need to be cautious was not that vital. After that, as the big hunt was underway, hundreds of police officers were patrolling the streets in the hope that, sooner or later, the criminal would fall under their hands. With its

brutality and lack of motivation, the crime on Osborne Street had the stamp of the Ripper on the case. There is a fact that the initial thought of police was that this victim was a victim of some of the Whitechapel blackmailing groups and there evidence to support this notion due to the fact that there was no evidence of money in the purse of the victim. However, it's more possible to be the case that Emma Smith was as penniless as she left her hotel the night before as she was when her body was discovered. An empty wallet was not something new to women of her kind. It's been a mystery to me that someone could be murdered for profit. In the case of robbery, as the motive the exact type of victim could be chosen...
"As in all cases of murder in the United States regardless of how poor or unfriendly the victim may be, the police took every step to find Emma Smith's attacker. Unlikely and likely areas were searched for clues. Many individuals were interrogated, most of them personally. A variety of confessions were taken. The soldiers of The Tower of London were questioned regarding their movement. The docks at ships were searched and sailors interrogated. This was all in vain. No clue was found. Nobody seemed to have seen the fatal blow strike or heard the sound, and no one was capable of describing the appearance of the man with whom the victim may be witnessed. There was silence and abruptness that it was completely void of evidence, and the bizarre disappearance all confirm

my belief that I have always believed to be true. Emma Smith was the first to be killed in the hands by Jack the Ripper. ... In the inquest hearings, the Coroner gave remarks that were strangely prophetic. After expressing his opinion on the brutality and mystery of the crime, the Coroner then expressed his displeasure at the prospect that a particularly brutal murderer still in the area. ... Other than the police, who were doing their best to locate the murderer The tragedy that was Emma Smith, the victim of the Osborne Street crime, was lost in the blink of an eye after her body was laid to rest in a pauper's tomb." The Chronicles of Crime and Criminals amazing criminal trials, unsolved murders, wholesale killings, female and male poisoners counterfeiting and forgery, banks and post-office robberies highway robbery, swindlers and railway crime (1895) that documented some of the most notorious crimes and described the initial reaction to the murder of Emma Smith by noting that Whitechapel was a shady poor area "The first installment of the Whitechapel murder series received very only a small amount of attention from the public. The crime was committed on the 3rd of April, 1888. This victim is Emma Elizabeth Smith. When the officer stooped over her, gazed into her face that was bloody, in the glow of bullseye, looked into her eyes with bleary eyes, smelled her breath soaked in gin, and examined her blood-stained clothing He reported the matter to the police

headquarters. The officers did not think too much with the incident. It was a girl of the lowest classes believed to be murdered in a drunken fight. What else would you expect from Whitechapel with its swarming number of criminals and slain women? The press made a few comments about the incident. The clubman laughed after reading about it during his meal while the lovely lady said it was shocking when she was frying her muffins for breakfast. And then the subject was brushed aside."
Given the fact that such a tragic ending was not unusual for working women in the East End, the murder was not a huge media splash. The Morning Advertiser reported very in the real sense, "Mr. Wynne Baxter conducted on Saturday morning on the London Hospital, an inquiry into the causes of the death of a tragic girl, named Emma Eliza Smith, who was attacked with the most brutal force at around 5:00 am on the Tuesday in the area of Osborn Street, Whitechapel. -- Mary Russell, the deputy-keeper of a popular lodging-house located within George- street, Spitalfields and stated that the deceased woman, who been in the home, left home on Monday night in good health. She returned between 4 and 5 the next day, suffering horrendous injuries. The woman testified that she had been horribly unwell-treated by a few men and then robbed. The woman's face was bleeding, and her ear was cut. Witness rushed her into the London Hospital, passing through Osborn-street in

the process and passing by a place that was close to a chocolate factory that Smith declared to be the spot where the savage act was committed. Smith was hesitant to give any further specifics, refused to explain the men or give any additional details of the incident to the witness. - Dr. G.H. Hillier who was the house surgeon present on Tuesday morning when the deceased patient was taken into the hospital, stated that the injuries that the woman sustained were awful. A part of her right ear was ripped and there was rupture of the peritoneum as well as other organs of the body, caused by a sharp instrument. The story of the incident, as told by the woman who suffered from the incident to her physician, is that it occurred around half-past-one-o'clock on a Tuesday morning, close to Whitechapel Church, she crossed across the road in order to stay clear of a group of men who followed her, brutally assaulted her, took of the entire amount she owned, and later did the heinous act. There were three or two males, one who looked like a young man of around nineteen. The patient passed away on Wednesday at around nine a.m. and was suffering from peritonitis...In answer to the questions of both the coroner as well as jurors, the physician stated that there was no doubt that the cause of death was through the wounds. The other organs to be in a good condition. The deceased claimed that she was from the country but she hadn't seen her family or friends in ten years. A second woman was later interviewed as a witness was found to have confessed to have seen Smith at about quarter-past 12 in the morning on Tuesday, close to the Burdett-road. They were talking to a man in dark clothing, wearing a white neckerchief around his neck. She was assaulted just within a couple of minutes prior to seeing Smith and was moving away from the neighborhood and was involved in some rough work done that night. Two people had come towards her, one of them asking for the time, and the other striking her with a smack and both escaping. She didn't think that the person who was talking with Smith might be one of her attackers. The man was Mr. John West, chief inspector of police for the H division, stated that there was no official record about the incident. He had asked the constables who were on duty in the Whitechapel-road at that time however none was aware of or witnessed the disturbances described in the report, or seen anyone being admitted to hospital. He made inquiries to Osborn-street based on the events that transpired during the inquiry. The Coroner, when the summation, said that based on the clinical evidence which has to be accurate it was evident that the woman was murdered, however who was the perpetrator? There was no evidence to prove. After a brief discussion and a verdict of "Wilful murder' for a particular individual or group of people was declared to jurors."

It was evident that she was murdered There was

hardly anything for the authorities to draw conclusions from because Smith was unable to identify the perpetrators and her past was unclear. Dew himself remarked, "Her past was a hidden book, even to her close acquaintances. The only thing she'd ever shared with anyone about her was the fact that she was widower who, more than ten years before had separated from her husband and walked away from her first relationships. It was something in Emma Smith which suggested that there was a time that the luxury of living were not denied to her. There was a hint of cultural influence in her words that was unusual for her class. When Emma was asked about why she was able to break apart so completely from her former life, she responded slightly wistfully: "They could not comprehend now as much as they did at the time. I have to live my life somehow.'"

It wasn't until four months after Martha Tabram, the victim's second name was discovered Martha Tabram, was found on August 7, killed and mutilated that the hunt for a possible killer began with a fervor. The day after the murder, the London Morning Advertiser reported on what was to become the first of many gruesome murders, but the editor had no way of knowing what was coming and thus treated the story like any other about a murdered prostitute: "At about ten minutes to five o'clock yesterday morning John Reeves, who lives at 37, George-yard-buildings, Whitechapel, was coming downstairs to go to work when he discovered the body of a woman lying in a pool of blood on the first-floor landing. Reeves summoned Constable Barrett, 26 H who was on the case near George-yard and his colleague Dr. Keeling, of Brick-lane was informed and arrived promptly. He immediately performed an exam of the woman and declared her dead and stated as his opinion that she was been brutally killed, there being knife wounds to her stomach, breasts and stomach. The body was the body of a woman, was around 5ft. 3in. in height, skin tone and hair were dark. She wore the dark green skirt with a brown petticoat the long black jacket and an afro-bonnet. The woman was not known to anyone who lives in one of the tenements located on the land where the body was discovered as no noise whatsoever was observed throughout the night. The body was transported into the Whitechapel mortuary, and the Inspector Elliston from the Commercial-street police station, put the case in the care of Inspector Reid who was a member of the Criminal Investigation Department. The building's superintendent was a block of model homes."

The article continued to provide a statement from witnesses Francis Hewitt as saying, "When I was summoned this morning, just before five o'clock, i saw the woman sitting on the stone stairs in a state of bleeding from a large wound on her heart. There were many more inflicted stab wounds that were of a frightening nature on her. At half-past-three this morning, some of the people in the room walked up the staircase which is why the murder was likely to have occurred later, as the victim was not present when the incident occurred. It is my opinion that the victim slipped through the stairs, that she was accompanied by a male in a dispute, which was fought over, and the man then stabbed her. Although the deceased isn't well-known but her face is well-known. It is likely that she was an unloved female."

The newspaper's initial descriptions were not enough to convey the horrific wounds were. The stabbing wounds to Tabram's body shocked the streets, which had become hard. One anonymous writer, who is believed to have access to her body, or even to the records of those who had write "But more shocking than the horrendous work on the neck was the realization that the victim had suffered at least thirty-nine distinct, clear and deep puncture wounds on different parts in her body. The blood was leaking out into her clothing, infusing her with blood and over the steps where she was lying with an impervious layer of blood coagulation. Examining this body showed the exact brutal mutilation to the uterus, which had been the hallmark of this murder as the initial one. The unclothing made of coarse material was thrown up over the victim's head , and it was a sharp wound that ran across the bowels, showing the intestinal tracts. Under this, a part of the woman's body been cut off using the grace and skill of a surgeon's knife with only blood-oozing an opening that was twitching. The organ was removed just like the initial murder. The police were in shock upon seeing the sight. The victim's friends were detained and taken to the coroner. There was not much evidence to shed light on the incident."

Doctor. Timothy Killeen arrived at the scene of the crime shortly before Tabram's body had been moved. He then examined the body at the mortuary. According to a story released by The East London Advertiser on August 11, "He had since made an post-mortem examination and upon opening the head, discovered that there was an swelling of red blood that was forming between his scalp and bone. Brain tissue was paler, however well-maintained... There was food during digestive process inside the stomach. Doctor. Keeling then described where the wounds were created and in response to questions, stated that there was no evidence of a recently a connection. He believed that these wounds could have been caused by knives or similar instrument but there was a cut on the chest bone, which may not be the result of knives. A penknife from the ordinary might have created the majority of the wounds, however the wound in the chest had to be caused by the bayonet of a sword or dagger. The wounds, according to his opinion, were caused through life and it was inconceivable to believe that all of them could be self-inflicted although some might be. In response to the coroner's questions regarding his ability to discern if the injuries were done by a left or left-handed individual, the doctor suggested that some of them could be the work of an left-handed person but not the other."

When the body was being scrutinized for clues, the police focused their attention on potential suspects and clients. Dew conducted interviews with a few residents in the area. Later, he reported, "One couple, a Mr. and Mrs. Mahoney returned at two at a.m. at dawn. They found nothing out of the ordinary. There was silence in the dull building until around an hour after, Albert Crow, whose work as a taxi driver been keeping him up late, returned home and took the stairs in a gruelling fashion. The dawn was breaking. In the light that filtered through the landing window Mr. Crow saw something on the wall. He stepped closer and realized that it was an elderly woman. She was lying across her rear. If it wasn't the day following the public holiday, Mr. Crow might have made an even more thorough investigation. However, after jumping into conclusions that this lady had enjoyed a party too much and was drunk to sleep, he went back to his home without giving it a second thought. ... In the same apartment in the same building was an individual named Reeves. She was asleep early, but was unable to get to sleep. She felt an unsettling sense of foreboding. At least three times, she woke her husband up and expressed her worries to him. He

laughed, rolled over, and fell back to sleep. However, the specter of the tragedy was so pervasive within Mrs. Reeves' mind that at about five o'clock, she had her husband awake yet again. The rage of her was so intense that the husband purely to pacify the situation, decided to look into the matter. He was still unsure as he made his way down the steps however, when he got to the first floor, he noticed something that was now clearly visible by the light of dawn which sucked the look of disbelief out of his face, and made him scramble to find an officer. P.C. Barrett was one of the officers he spotted. Together , they returned to the building. Though he was traumatized due to his police experience in Whitechapel the scene in where the police officer had been tackled totally frightened him, just like later, I was awed by the horrible incident that I witnessed in the tiny room of Miller's Court."
The main target of the police's first investigation were soldiers stationed in the close Tower of London. In the words of Dew, "It was known that Martha Turner had been in the habit of frequenting public houses in low places with sailors and soldiers. The first investigations were conducted among the sailors of the various docks as well as the soldiers who were stationed at Tower of London. Then , what appeared to be an affirmation of this idea. One of the victim's friends claimed that that night, the day of the murder she gone to Martha to a soldier near George Yard. ... the person who provided us with this information and was

later proved to be ineffective and was identified by the name of Pearly Poll. The story she told was that she spent the night along with Martha Turner, and that at 11 o'clock, they had encountered two soldiers. They stayed together until close to midnight, when Pearly and her friend walked away to leave Martha and her soldier companion out of the area where the murder occurred. This evidence cannot be ignored. In hoping that she might be capable of identifying two officers, Pearly Poll was taken to the Tower of London, where all the soldiers who were stationed there were paraded in front of her. Pearly was unable to identify the two soldiers, however being aware of the difficulty in identifying any person at any time particularly when it comes to soldiers wearing uniforms, the police were still hopeful they were on the right path. The the fact that a soldier likely have been wearing a bayonet, which is a weapon which injuries could have been inflicted to suggest the same direction."

At at this point, Dew was certain that Tabram was murdered with a killer who was serial and he pointed out the time of her death as a clue to link Smith's death to Tabram's "Then came the first concrete proof that Whitechapel was a home for the devil as a human. Emma Smith had been murdered on Easter Monday. The Ripper returned on the August Bank Holiday of the same year. This is a curious coincidence. Could it be that the two nights were planned? Do the fact that people from in the East End were on holiday somehow aid in the murders? Whatever you think about the murder of Emma Smith there can be no doubt that the August Bank Holiday murder, which occurred at the George Yard Buildings, less than a hundred yards away from the scene where the first victim was killed was the result of the notorious Ripper."

The passing of Mary Ann Nicholls on September 1 only heightened the police department's worries and fears, since her death appeared to confirm the worst fears of everyone that a madman was in the wild. Police Constable John Neil who, like the other constables who were stationed within Whitechapel, along with the other officers stationed in Whitechapel area, was on high alert, gave further details of what he witnessed: "Yesterday morning I was going through Buck's-row, Whitechapel, going toward Brady-street. There was nobody around. I had been the area for about an hour earlier but I didn't see one. The street was empty, and I was walking on the right end of the block and I saw a body sitting on the street. It was dark but there was a street light shining towards near the bottom of the row. I walked across to find the body of a deceased woman lying in front of a gateway with her head to the east. The gateway was shut. It was around nine or ten feet in height and led to stables. There were homes from the east side of the gate as well as there was the School Board school occupies the westward part of the road. On the other end of the roadway lies Essex Wharf. The deceased was lying in a long line along the street with her left hand reaching out to the gate. ... Then I could hear an officer walking by Brady-street, and I called him. I didn't whistle. I told him to "Run as fast as you can to the doctor. Llewellyn,' and when I saw another constable at Baker's-row I directed him to an ambulance. The doctor arrived in extremely short amount of time. In the time, rung the alarm on Essex Wharf, and asked whether there was any noise noticed. The answer was 'No. Sergeant Kirby was next and knocked. ... Surrounding the corpse was an uncut piece of comb and some looking-glass. The body was not found with money and a unmarked white handkerchief was discovered inside her pocket."

The first issue naturally, was whether Neil had met anyone that could be the killer. Neil insisted that, as he was running his beat, "I heard nothing. The furthest I'd been in the night was through the Whitechapel-road up Baker's-row. I never strayed far from the place. I saw many women along the main road heading back home. At that point, anyone could have been able to escape. ... Then I surveyed the road, but could not notice the marks of wheels. The first people to arrive at the scene when I found bodies were two people who worked in a slaughterhouse next to. They stated that they were unaware about the incident and claimed that they didn't hear any screaming. I've seen them before, and they were men working. This would be around an hour and a quarter or a half-hour before I discovered the body."

In the later inquiry at the inquest, Dr. Henry Llewellyn described the injuries in details, which he had been taught to do. He informed the coroner's jury, "Five of the teeth are missing and there's a minor cut on the tongue. The right-hand side of his face, there is a laceration that runs along the lower portion of the jaw. It could be caused by an impact by the fist or pressure exerted by the thumb. On the left face, there was a circular cut which could also be caused by the force of fingers. The left-hand side of the neck approximately one inch below the jawline there is an opening approximately four inches wide and extending from an area directly beneath the ear. One inch below, on the same side and beginning approximately 1 inch in front of it the incision was circular, ending at a point approximately 3" below jaw's right. The incision totally sever all tissues into the vertebrae. The big vessels in cervical necks on the two sides were cut off. The cut is approximately eight inches in length. The incisions must have been made with an extended-bladed knife that was moderately sharp and made with a lot of force. The blood was not discovered on the breasts, either in the human body, or on clothing. There were no wounds on the body up to the lower portion in the abdominal area. A couple of inches away from the left side, there was a wound which was jagged. It was a deeply cut wound and the tissues were cut. There were numerous cuts through the abdominal area. The right-hand side, there were four or three similar cuts that were running downwards. These were all created by the use of a knife that had been used with violence and was utilized downwards. The injuries ranged from left to right and could have been caused by a left-handed man. The injuries were performed using an instrument of the same type."

The next day, after Nicholls was discovered dead The London Times reported at length about the circumstances surrounding her death "Another murder of the most vile kind took place in the vicinity that is Whitechapel during the wee hours the morning yesterday however, who was responsible and what motives are currently a mystery. About a quarter-hour before 4 o'clock , police-constable Neill of 97J, who was in the Buck's-row area of Whitechapel found an unidentified woman's body lying in an area of the footway as he stooped to lift her in the hope that she was drunk , he discovered that her throat had been cut from ear to. She was dead , but warm. He sought assistance and was immediately was taken to the station as well as an ambulance. The doctor, Dr. Llewellyn, of Whitechapel-road and whose office is more than 300 yards from the place the woman was lying in a coma, was agitated by the request by a constable, was dressed and immediately went on the spot. He examined the body near the location in which it was located and declared that the victim was dead. He conducted a quick examination and found out that, aside from the gash that was across the throat, the lady was suffering from severe injuries to the abdomen. The ambulance of the police of the Bethnal-green Station having arrived, the body was taken to the Bethnal-green Station. Further examination revealed the terrible nature of the crime. there were numerous horrific gashes and cuts, one was severe enough to cause death, in addition to the cuts across the throat."

Buck's Row, where Nicholls was killed.
Being certain that they had the serial killer, police were quick to attempt to locate any evidence that could help in stopping the murderer. The story continued "After the corpse was moved to the funeral home of the parish in Old Montague Street, Whitechapel the police took steps to ensure, if it was

it was possible, identification, however initially with no chance of being successful. The clothes were that of a typical description and it was the skirt that one of them wore as well as the band of a different petticoat had the stamp that was ascribed to Lambeth Workhouse. The only things found inside those pockets was a hair comb as well as an eye glass. This latter item led the investigators to determine that the dead woman was a resident in one of one of the many lodges of the area, and police were sent to investigate regarding, and other officers who went to Lambeth to request an employee of the working house in order to look at the body in order to identifying. However, the latter was unable to identify the body the victim, and claimed that the clothing could be issued at any point in the last several years. When the word of the murder spread the first woman, and later another, arrived to examine the body. At the end of the day, it was discovered that a woman who matched her description as the murder woman was staying in a standard lodging house at 18, Thrawl-street in Spitalfields. Women from the area were located and confirmed the dead as being 'Polly' who shared the same room with three females in the house in the normal manner of such homes -- a weekly payment of 4d. each, each lady having an individual bed...It was discovered that the deceased lived the lifestyle of an "unlucky one' in the house, and it was for just three weeks. There was nothing more known about the deceased by the police, except the fact that when she showed up for lodging on a Thursday night, she was rejected by the officer because she was not able to pay. Then she was the worst in terms of drinking, but was she was not drunk and walked off laughing, saying "I'll soon receive my doss' cash and see what a fun bonnet I've got. She was wearing a bonnet that was not seen before and left the house at the front door. The woman in the neighborhood observed her afterward and told the police at 2:30 in the Friday morning, in Whitechapel-road. It was close to the church and at the intersection of Osborne-street and at around four she was discovered within 500 yards from the spot, murdered."In the wake of Nicholls the death of Nicholls the police appeared to be able to make a breakthrough in the case of witnesses Henry Birch, who owned a dairy near the spot the spot where she was murdered was some of the first description of the perpetrator. The media reported that "Not more than a quarter past eleven, a man made his way into the front yard of the address. 2, Little Turner Street, Commercial-road. On the other corner of the garden is a stand for milk. The man requested an ice-cold glass of milk and, after being served, consumed it quickly before, while looking around in a panicked manner and asked to return to the yard. The owner, Henry Birch, did not object, however in the midst of his fears being triggered when he saw the man and saw him wearing a set of new overalls over normal clothing. Pants were in place, and he was trying to remove an outfit from a shiny bag on his feet when Birch approached him. He appeared to be annoyed by the interruption and at first, he was unable to speak. Then he declared, "That was a terrible murder that happened last night, wasn't it?" Before Birch could respond, he stated, "I think I've got an idea," and, snatching the bag from his hand and vanishing in the streets. He was. Birch then thought he might have been a detective using disguises for some motive, but the police believe he was actually the person who attacked the woman at Cambridge Heath-road and that he wore the overalls in order to confuse anyone trying to trace the suspect. The police have identified the identity of the lady they refer to, as well as her description that matches that of Birch of the mysterious caller. The attire was called a blue serge outfit as well as a stiff and low-pitched hat. He wore a collar that was stand-up as well as the watch-chain. He did not have a beard but had a dark, slight moustache. His face appeared to be sun-burned. Birch states that he thought that he was a sea-going person or was recently on a long trip. As soon as he put the overalls , he had the appearance like an engineer. A lot of the details in this description are identical to those by the man who made these shrewd inquiries regarding women in the Nuns Head Tavern, Aldgate on the night of Saturday as well as to a different report from the police and are inclined to tie the man's name to the most recent killings." The media largely did not report on the story of Birch, and since he didn't see the face of the man however, he was unable draw any kind of solid identity of the suspect. But the police did file his information as they began their desperate search for the murderer.

Police were plagued during the investigation due to the killer's capacity to flee the scene that he was executing his attack without being discovered, which suggests that Jack the Ripper was quite well-known to the area. However, while there was nothing they could do to stop this but there was the issue regarding how information was dealt with and continued to be an problem. This negligence resulted in The Daily Telegraph to report on September 3, 1888, about the consequences of such inattention.

"Mr. Wynne"Mr. Wynne. Baxter is the coroner of South-East Middlesex, yesterday [3 September] resumed his investigation in the Work Lads' Institute at Whitechapel-road, on the circumstances leading to the murder of woman Mary Ann Nicholls .... The Inspector John Spratling, J Division was questioned about when he first was informed of the crime around half-past-four on Friday morning when he was at Hackney-road. Witnesses said that he then was able to see the body as it was taken off.

Detective-sergeant Enright The incident was uncovered by two of the prison officials.

The Coroner: Did they have any authority to remove

the body?
Witness the witness: No, sir. I did not give them any instructions to take it off. In fact, I instructed the witnesses to keep it the way it was.
A Coroner's Statement: I do not protest against them stripping their body, but it is important to have proof of the clothes.
Sergeant Enright continued, saying the clothes, being thrown out within the garden, comprised of an ulster in reddish-brown with seven brass buttons and an ecru dress that appeared brand like it was brand new. Also, there was two flannel and wool dress, which belonged of the Workhouse. The inspector Helson had cut pieces that were marked "P. R., Princes-road," with a intention of tracing the body. Also, there was two stays in good condition, however the witness did not observe the manner in which they had been adjusted."
There were no photos of the scene of the crime, Baxter was relying on eyewitness testimony regarding what was the state of Nicholls' clothing that were worn at the time Nicholls was discovered. The story was further outlined:
"The Coroner has said that he believed it vital to know the exact condition where the remains were discovered.
Based on the advice from Inspector Aberline garments were seized.
The Foreman of the jury inquired whether the stays

had been fastened to the body.

Inspector Spratling stated that he was unable to confirm. The blood was evident on the top of the dress's body and on the ulster. However, Inspector Spratling only saw a tiny amount under-linen and it could have occurred after the body was removed from Buck's-row. The clothes were secured at the time he first observed the body. The stays didn't stay in place very well, since the man could look at the wounds, without taking them off. them."

Investigators might have thought they knew the dangers they faced following Nicholls murder However, the speed of the murders was set to accelerate."

Chapter 3: The Investigation

The vast majority of City of London Cops submits related in their inquiry into Whitechapel murders were destroyed during the Blitz. The timeless Metropolitan Cops submits enable an deep understanding of the methods used to investigate during The Victorian period. A large group of officers answered house-to-house queries in Whitechapel. Forensic evidence was collected and looked at. Criminals were identified, followed and then taken for an examination or excluded from the investigation. Modern police work follows exactly the same procedure. Over 2,000 people were interrogated, "upwards of 300" people were questioned and more than 80 were detained. After the deaths of Stride and Eddowes The Commissioner of City Cops, Sir James Fraser provided a reward worth five hundred British pounds for the capture of Jack the Ripper.

The investigation was initially conducted in The Metropolitan Authorities Whitechapel (H) Division Lawbreaker Examination Department (CID) led by the Investigator Inspector Edmund Reid. After the death of Nichols Investigator Inspectors Frederick Abberline, Henry Moore as well as Walter Andrews were sent out from Headquarters at Scotland Garden to help. They were also part of the City of London Authorities were joined by Detective Inspector James McWilliam after the Eddowes murder, which occurred in the City of London. The direction of the killing inquiries was hindered because the newly appointed chief of the CID Robert Anderson was on leave in Switzerland between September 7th through the 6th of October, during the period when Chapman, Stride, and Eddowes were killed. This led Metropolitan Authorities Commissioner Sir Charles Warren to choose the Chief Inspector Donald Swanson to collaborate the investigation in Scotland Garden.

Butchers, slaughterers and cosmetic surgeons, and physicians were thought to be responsible for the manner in which they mutilated themselves. A note of investigation by Significant Henry Smith, Acting Commissioner of the City Authorities, suggests that the abstentions of regional butchers as well as slaughterers were scrutinized, and which led to the conclusion that they were cleared of the search. The report of inspector Swanson in the Office confirms that 76 slaughterers and butchers were removed from the list the inquiry, and included all of their employees for the past six months. A few contemporary figures, including Queen Victoria believed that they could see that the sequence of murders indicated that the murderer was either a livestock driver or butcher in one of the boats for livestock which sailed across London with mainland Europe. Whitechapel was situated close near the London Docks, and typically these boats docked on Thursday or Friday , and departing on Saturday or Sunday. The boats that were used for livestock were examined however the date of the murders weren't accompanied by any boat's movement, or the transfer of a crew member to boats also ruled out.

Whitechapel Alertness Committee

In the month of September, 1888, a group volunteers living in the London's East End formed the Whitechapel Alertness Committee. They scoured the streets for suspicious individuals, partly due to their displeasure at the inability of the police to catch the perpetrator as well as because some members were worried that the murders could affect the services offered in the area. The Committee asked for the Federal government to increase an incentive for information leading to an arrest for the murderer they also offering their own reward of L 50 in exchange for information that led to the capture of the killer, and hired private investigators to investigate witnesses on their own.

The Criminal Profiling

In the month of October, at the end, Robert Anderson

asked cops cosmetic surgeon Thomas Bond to give his perspective on the killer's surgical skill and expertise. The view that was offered by Bond regarding the nature that is"the "Whitechapel Killer" is the oldest surviving transgressor's profile. Bond's assessment was based on his own evaluation of the most severely injured victim and postmortem notes of the four previous canonical murders. Bond wrote:

Each of the five murders was executed by the same person. In the first four cases the throats are believed to be cutting from the left side to the right. In the final case due to the massive mutilation it's difficult to tell where the fatal cut was made. However, blood vessels were found on the wall in a few splashes close to the spot where the woman's head ought to be lying.

The numerous scenarios surrounding the murders have led me to think that the victims should be lying down when they were killed and, in each case, the throat was cut first.

Mr. Bond was strongly opposed to the notion that the murderer was a person with any kind of physical or clinical knowledge as well as "the technical skills of an animal slaughterer or butcher". According to him the murderer was a man who had a unique routine, and who was subject to "periodical attacks of sensual and bloodthirsty mania" as well as the style of the mutilations could suggest "satyriasis". Mr. Bond said that "the bloodthirsty instinct could be a result of a vengeful or brooding state of the mind, or a spiritual mania may have been the cause, but I don't think either is likely".

There is no evidence that the perpetrator was involved in sexual sex with any one of the victims. However, psychologists think that the cutting of the victims by knives and "leaving the victims exposed in sexually degrading postures with the wounds exposed" suggests that the perpetrator enjoyed sexual pleasure from the attack. This interpretation of the event is not accepted by some who dismiss such notions as unacceptable beliefs.

Apart from the absurdities and inconsistency of contemporary stories, efforts to determine the perpetrator are hampered by the lack of legal evidence. DNA analysis on letters from the past is not certain; the evidence available has been scrutinized numerous times, and is contaminated to provide substantial results. There have been contradictory assertions that DNA proves definitively to two different suspects. The method of both has been attacked.

Suspects

The deliberate discussion of the murders during holidays and weekends, and within a small distance from one another has led many to believe they believe that Ripper was working in a routine job and was in the area. Some have suggested that the murderer was an educated upper-class person possibly a doctor or aristocrat who walked to Whitechapel coming from more affluent region. These theories rely on social conceits like the fears of the health profession as well as skepticism towards modern research, or the exploitation of the poor and marginalized by the rich. The suspects suggested following the killings comprise almost anyone who is remotely linked to the investigation by modern documents, as well as a number of popular names that were not thought of in investigation by the authorities, such as but not restricted to part of the British royal family as well as an artist and a physician. Everyone alive at the time has passed away and writers of the present can indict anyone "with no need of historical proof". The suspects in contemporary police dossiers include three in Sir Melville Macnaghten's 1894 memorandum. the evidence against them is, at the very least, circumstantial.

There are a variety of divergent theories on the identity and job of Jack the Ripper However, the authorities haven't in agreement on any of them. In fact, the number of suspects who are being investigated is more than 100. Despite the continuing interest in the incident the identity of the Ripper remains unknown. "Ripperology," as it is known "ripperology" was coined to refer to the analysis and study of the Ripper cases. The killings have inspired many fictional works.

Letters

In the course of the Whitechapel murders, police along with the papers and people received a variety of letters about the incident. A few of the letters were well-intentioned and offered of tips on how to identify the murderer however, the vast majority were either scams or useless.

Many letters are believed to be composed by the murderer himself and 3 of them particularly are in high demand: The "Dear Boss" letter and "Saucy Jackie" postcard "Saucy Jacky" postcard, and the "From Hell" letter.

The "Dear Boss" letter, sent on the 25th, and mailed September 27th, of 1888. It was discovered on that afternoon by Central News Agency, and was delivered to Scotland Garden on 29 September. Initially, it was thought to be a fraud however, when Eddowes was discovered 3 days after the date of the letter's postmark, with one ear cut in a slender manner off her body promise that the writer would "clip the girl's (sic) ears" attracted attention. Eddowes's ear is believed to have been damaged by the murderer in a method he carried out his attack and the letter's risk of releasing the ears to authorities was never carried out. The title "Jack The Ripper" was first utilized in this letter by the person who signed it and gained worldwide recognition after the publication. Most of the letters that followed followed the tone of this letter. There are sources that claim that a note dated 17 September in 1888 was the first letter to utilize"Jack The Ripper" "Jack the Ripper", however most experts believe it was a false statement that was later inserted into police records during the early 20th century.

"Saucy Jacky" postcard "Saucy Jacky" postcard was sent out on October 1st, 1888, and was received on the same day by the Central News Agency. The handwriting is reminiscent of similar to the "Dear Boss" letter, and also discussed the canonical murders that occurred on September 30 and 30 September, as the writer explains in writing "double events the second time". It was suggested that this postcard had been printed prior to the murders being made public which makes it unlikely that a crank could have any knowledge of the criminal act. However, it was sent out over 24 hours after the murders occurred and was published long after the details of the murders had been discovered and reported by journalists and was then absorbed into social chatter among the people of Whitechapel.

"From Hell" letter "From Hell" letter was received through George Lusk, leader of the Whitechapel Alertness Committee, on October 16th of the year 1888. The style of writing and handwriting is different from "Saucy Jackie" and the "Dear Boss" letter as well as the "Saucy Jacky" postcard. The letter came in an unassuming box inside which Lusk discovered the kidney of a human which was preserved with "spirits from red wine" (ethanol). The left kidney of Eddowes was eliminated by the murderer. The author claimed that the killer "fried and then ate" the kidney that was missing. There is a debate over the kidney. Some say that it was a gift from Eddowes and others believe it was an obscene incident. The kidney was studied by Dr. Thomas Openshaw of the London Medical facility. He confirmed that it was human and was from the left side. However, (contrary the incorrect reports on paper) the doctor was unable to determine any other characteristics that are natural to humans. Openshaw therefore also received an official letter from "Jack the Ripper".

Scotland Garden released facsimiles of the "Dear

Boss" letter and postcard on the 3rd of October with the hopes that a member of the general public would recognize the handwriting. Charles Warren clarified in a letter addressed to Godfrey Lushington, Permanent Under-Secretary of State for the Home Department: "I think that the whole thing is a fraud however we'll investigate and determine who wrote it in any event." On the 7th of October in the year 1888 George R. Sims in the Sunday newspaper Referee claimed with a scathing tone it was the work of a journalist "to send the circulation of blood on an article to the skies". Police authorities later claimed to that they had identified a specific reporter was the one who wrote each of the "Dear Boss" letter as well as the postcard. The reporter was identified to be Tom Bullen in a letter from Chief Inspector John Littlechild to George R. Sims that was sent on September 23rd, 1913. A reporter named Fred Best supposedly admitted in 1931 that the two of them at The Star had written the letters with the signature "Jack The Ripper" to draw attention to the murders and to "keep the business going".

Chapter 4: The Limelight

The Ripper murders are a significant moment in the way we deal with criminal activities by journalists. Jack the Ripper wasn't the first serial murderer, but his story was the first one to cause an all-over world media frenzy. It was the Elementary Education Act in the year 1880 (which was an extension of an earlier Act) mandated that school attendance obligatory regardless of the class. In the year 1888, more people of working class living in England as well as Wales were educated.

Tax reforms of the 1850s made it possible to publish cheap papers with a greater circulation of blood. They exploded in the late Victorian time period, with mass-circulation papers that cost just a halfpenny and famous publications such as The Illustrated Authorities News that led to the Ripper the subject of extraordinary publicity. Then, during the peak investigations, more than one million copies that included a comprehensive report on the Whitechapel murders were purchased each day. However, many of the stories were sensationalistic or speculation, and inaccurate information was frequently published as factual. Furthermore, some of the articles that speculated on what the real identity was of the Ripper included rumors of regional xenophobia that the killer was Jewish or from another country.

In the beginning of September, six days following the death of Mary Ann Nichols, The Manchester Guardian stated: "Whatever info could be at the disposal of authorities, they believe it is necessary to hide ... It's believed that their focus is focused on ... an unpopular character known as "Leather Apron'." Reporters were irritated by the insistence to the CID to reveal the details about their probe to public, and thus resorted to writing reports that were doubtful of accuracy. Ingenious explanations about "Leather Apron" were published in the media and other media, however competing journalists rejected them as "a famous fad of the reporter's imagination". John Pizer, a regional Jew who made shoes out of leather, was referred to by the moniker "Leather Apron" and was in jail, but the inspector who examined him said that "at the moment, there is no evidence whatsoever against him". He was released shortly after the confirmation of his Alibis.

Following the publication of the "Dear Boss" letter, "Jack the Ripper" was replaced by "Leather Apron" as the term used by the media and the public to describe the murderer. The term "Jack" was previously used to refer to another famous London adversary "Spring-heeled Jack", who appeared to leap over walls to strike his victims and escape quickly as fast as he could. The ingenuity and the use of a term to describe an individual killer ended up being a standard practice in the media with examples such as those of Axeman from New Orleans, the Boston Strangler as well as the Beltway Sniper. The examples that come of Jack the Ripper are the French Ripper, the Dusseldorf Ripper, the Camden Ripper, the Blackout Ripper, Jack the Stripper, the Yorkshire Ripper as well as the Rostov Ripper. The shocking press coverage combined with the fact that no one was ever proven guilty of the murders have left academics puzzled and created a mythology that casts a shadow on the serial killers of the future.

In the case of Ripper murders and the low life style of the victims amplified the squalor of life in the East End and galvanised popular opinions against the overcrowded, insalubrious shanty towns. Within the two decades following the murders, some of the worst neighborhoods have been destroyed and cleared however, the streets and a few structures survive and the story of the Ripper is promoted in numerous guided trips to the sites of murder and other sites that refer to the incident. In the past it was The 10 Bells pub in Commercial Street (which was often visited by at minimum one of the legendary Ripper victim) was the subject of these trips.

In the immediate aftermath of the murders, and later, "Jack the Ripper ended becoming the children's"bogeyman." The representations were typically phantasmic or terrifying. The 1920s, 1930s

Ripper was depicted in films wearing everyday clothes as a person with a hidden agenda, profiting from his unsuspecting clients; the environment and his evil were portrayed by shadows and lighting. By the 1960s, Ripper was "the symbol of the prey-oriented higher society" and was frequently seen in a stovepipe cap that disguised as a gentleman. The Facility as a whole was portrayed as the villain and the Ripper acting as a sign of the oppression of the upper classes. Ripper's image was Ripper is a combination of images from horror films like Dracula's cape and the organ of Victor Frankenstein. The reality of Ripper may be merged with a variety of kinds of categories, in scope from Sherlock Holmes up to Japanese sexual terror. Jack the Ripper appears in a variety of stories of fiction as well as pieces that blur the boundaries between fiction and fact, which comprises the Ripper letters as well as an untrue journal called The Journal of Jack the Ripper. The Ripper is in books and narratives, poetry comics, games, musicals and plays, as well as operas as well as tv shows and even in movies. More than a hundred non-fiction books deal exclusively dealing with Jack the Ripper. Jack the Ripper murders, making it among the most popular true crime subjects to be written about. "The term "ripperology" was invented in the 1970s by Colin Wilson in the 1970s to describe the study of the case conducted by professionals and amateurs. The periodic publications Ripperana, Ripperologist, and Ripper Notes publish their research.

In 2006 an BBC History publication survey picked Jack the Ripper as the most vile Briton in all of history.

In 2015 in 2015, in 2015, the Jack The Ripper Museum was opened in East London. The museum was criticized by the Tower Hamlets mayor John Biggs as well as protestors. Similar demonstrations took place in 2021 after the second of two "Jack The Chipper" fish and chip shops opened in Greenwich and some customers threatened to boycott the establishment. There isn't a waxwork model that resembles Jack the Ripper at Madame Tussauds' Chamber of Horrors, contrary to other killers that are less popular and in line with their rule of never modeling people who have a similarity that is not identified. Instead, he is depicted as shadow.

Chapter 5: Let's see if we can form a Visual

"First Let's look at if we can create an image of what the characteristics of killer like Jack the Ripper could be. The question will help us to identify the man we determined to be. First of all the man would not be extremely old or young or very old, since he would not have had the experience that would have led to such an obsession as his. not old enough, because the fact that he wouldn't have the power or ability, nor courage to commit this kind of a string of crimes. What were the circumstances that could trigger this type of obsession? It is imperative to note that the mania for murdering women from the class that were victim of Jack the Ripper isn't unique. ... It is believed that the root motive behind this type of mania is the destruction of the mind brought on by a constitutional illness and the need to bring revenge on the class that was believed to be spring. This is among the many reasons that indicate the fact that Jack the Ripper would be someone who is past the age of years of age, and would endure years of extreme physical and mental. It is commonly observed that the concept of contracting the disease, despite being not true, causes the same type of manic depression." The Sun 13 February 1894.

Nearly 120 years have passed since the Ripper's crime rampage, there is still a lot of controversy over the fact that Mary Jane Kelly was the final victim to the serial killer. Hence, it shouldn't be a surprise that, even after the last canonical murder was executed, police and others continued to look into and speculate about who the Ripper could be. Naturally, there was no group more passionate in the investigation of the murderer than London's press.

On the 13th February 1894, a few years following the Whitechapel murders were over, The Sun of London surprised its readers by the name of the suspect of its very own. The article laid the basis to support its claim by saying, "Just three years have been passed since these murders stopped taking place and this interruption in the string of crimes is a clear indication of the disappearance, in one way or another of the person who was the culprit. However, besides the possibility of the possibility of detection - which hasn't occurred - or even death there is another option. These injuries can only be performed by a psychotic homicidal maniac; and a homicidal maniac may occasionally attempt murder but not succeed; inflicting possibly an injury, and sometimes creating a fear, and being caught in these relatively minor crimes and proving to be insane, can be locked up, with no making a fuss, or attracting the attention of anyone or even receiving a mention in the newspaper. ... That's what was the result with regard to Jack the Ripper. He was initially brought to jail on the suspicion of being a dangerous insane. ... in the legal brief of the lawyer who prosecuted, as well as in the direction of the lawyer who defended the case, was the exact declaration - that he had been believed to be Jack the Ripper. ... It was immediately sent to the living grave in a mental asylum and there, he could be dead without any mention of his horrific secret if an accidental clue didn't have put a spokesman for The Sun on the track."

The reporter continued to recount a story that was which was said to be shared by a person referred to"WK "WK": "At 10.30 on a Saturday night in 1891 the man was seen walking around an abandoned building located within the North of London. It was close to an avenue through which trains run along, as well W K got out at this time with his love interest. While they were walking, the silhouette of a slim, tall young man walked by in darkness. He was extremely excited and a bit strange. The collar of his coat was turned towards his throat while his head was pulled across his face. He began to talk with them, asking they would keep him from being spotted since the runners were following the suspect and PS500 was given to him for his fear. When he spoke, an cab sped through and he yelled "There they come!" and walked up to the door of the house , and held the doorknocker as if he was about knock, but didn't. When he saw the cab pass and he walked out of the door and went to meet with Mr. K who attempted to calm him down and snort his worries but he was unable to be calmed. ... The man gave a lengthy and rambling speech with great force, stating that the police wanted him for a serious offense. "You should know," stated the judge, 'that people claim that I'm Jack the Ripper But I'm not, even though their intestines have been opened and their stomachs have been taken out. I am a doctor and you're aware of that, but I'm isn't Jack the Ripper You shouldn't think that I are. However, they are and they're looking for me. The runners are following me because they want the PS500 which they are offering to me for my capture. I've been merely cutting up women and then laying in.'"

The article also mentions WK himself as saying "I I THOUGHT HE WAS JACK The RIPPER. However, I didn't want to admit it in the moment, because I was not wanting to scare my lover. He spoke so many times in the two hours we talked that I'm not able to recall everything but I can remember that I was impressed when I was young with the impression of being Jack the Ripper. He stated that PS500 was given to his services, and then begged me to go to his home and keep him there. I was a little scared of him, but he pleaded to me so much that I was envious of him and was relieved not to to be a nuisance to him. I was able to discern from his comments that it was his medical field. After he left, I became curious and went after him, forming our minds that when we saw the policeman that we should charge him. We followed him along Camden street, through Georgians street, over Camden street, then to the Winkworth's wine shop near Bayham Wharf, where I was able to go down however he did not but I didn't see his absence completely."

The man named in the newspaper The Sun turned out to be Thomas Cutbush, a young medical student who was kept within Broadmoor Hospital since 1891 after his delusions started to take over him and tried to stab a couple of women in an infirmary prior to being voluntarily admitted into the hospital. Although The Sun offered several articles that provided "evidence" to Cutbush but the police didn't think he was a credible suspect. In fact the Sir Melville Macnaghten, who served as the Assistant Chief Constable of the Metropolitan Police during the period of the murders, was furious by the claims of The Sun that he signed an official memorandum in which he named his own suspects, however during this process, he clarified how the police previously dealt with Cutbush prior to that: "The case referred to in the thrilling story that was published in the newspaper "The Sun" in the 13th issue and subsequent dates is the one from Thomas Cutbush who was arraigned in the London County Sessions in April 1891, on the charge of intentionally wounding Florence Grace Johnson, and trying to injure Isabella Fraser Anderson in Kennington. He was found insane and was sentenced to detention for a time during the Pleasure of Her Majesty's. The case of Cutbush was a resident of his aunt and mother on fourteen Albert Street, Kennington, was released from Lambeth Infirmary. Lambeth Infirmary, (after he was detained for only two hours, for being an insane person) at noon on the 5th March 1891. The arrest was made on the 9th day. In the weeks before this, numerous instances of jabbing or stabbing from behind had been reported in the vicinity. In one of these cases, an individual named Colicott was detained but later released for an error in identification. The cuts on the dresses of the girl caused by Colicott were not like the cut(s) created by Cutbush (when he injured the victim, Miss Johnson) whom was in no doubt motivated by a intense desire for morbid imitators. ... They not possible to establish his movements during the nights during The Whitechapel murders. The knife that was discovered on him was purchased in Houndsditch just a few days before his detention in the Infirmary. Cutbush was the cousin of Supt. Executive."

The issue with Cutbush Macnaghten claims is that he didn't appear to be a violent enough person to be able to commit the crimes of the Ripper. "It is worth noting that the severity of the mutilations grew in every case, and evidently, the appetite was heightened by the indulgence. It is, therefore, very unlikely that the murderer had suddenly stopped his murder in the month of November, 1988, and then recommenced operations simply by poking a girl in the back for two years and four months later. Another more reasonable theory is that the killer's brain was a complete collapse after his terrible consumption at Miller's Court, and that the murderer immediately took his own life or, as an alternative it is possible that he was insanely mad by his family members that he was being held in an asylum."

Based on this assumption, Macnaghten went on to identify his own suspects, starting with "Mr M. J. Druitt who was believed that he was a medical doctor of a good family and who vanished in the aftermath that of Miller's Court murder. Miller's Court killing, and the body (which was reported to have been more than one year in the sea) was discovered within the Thames on the 31st of Decemberaround seven weeks after the murder. Druitt was sexually insane, and based on private information, I am confident that his family believed he had been the killer."

Montague John Druitt circa 1880

Macnaghten

some asylum.

No one ever saw the Whitechapel murderer; many homicidal maniacs were suspected, but no shadow of proof could be thrown on any one. I may mention the cases of 3 men, any one of whom would have been more likely than Cutbush to have committed this series of murders:—

(1) A Mr M. J. Druitt, said to be a doctor & of good family, who disappeared at the time of the Miller's Court murder, & whose body (which was said to have been upwards of a month in the water) was found in the Thames on 31st Dec:— or about 7 weeks after that murder. He was sexually insane and from private info I have little doubt but that his own family believed him to have been the murderer.

(2) Kosminski, a Polish Jew, resident in Whitechapel. This man became insane owing to many years indulgence in solitary vices. He had a great hatred of women, specially of the prostitute class, & had strong homicidal tendencies; he was removed to a lunatic asylum about March 1889. There were many circs connected with this man which made him a strong "suspect".

(3) Michael Ostrog, a Russian doctor, and a convict, who was subsequently detained in a lunatic asylum as a homicidal maniac. This man's antecedents were of the worst possible type, and his whereabouts at the time of the murders could never be ascertained.

A photo of a page where Macnaghten identifies the suspects

In reality, Druitt was a lawyer and assistant schoolmaster in London. Druitt had a lengthy family history of mental illness , and was believed to have committed suicide at some point after the demise of Mary Jane Kelly. Since Mary Jane Kelly was the final of the five canonical victims, and that many believe that she was the last of the Ripper's victims and that Druitt's suicide occurred near the conclusion of the Ripper's infamous crime spree was a bit in circumstantial proof. But, the majority of investigators did not agree with Macnaghten's conclusion and included inspector Frederick Abberline, who remarked, "But what does it really mean? It's as simple as this. After the last crime at Whitechapel an unidentified doctor was discovered in the Thames however, there is nothing more than the fact that the body was discovered in the Thames at that time to implicate the doctor. A report was sent by the Home Office about the matter however to say that it was "considered to be final and conclusive' is completely against the facts. Given that the same type of murders started in America afterward and that there was a good reason to believe that the victim moved to the United States. In addition it is interesting that, a few months later, in December 1888, the time that the student's body was discovered, the detectives were instructed to remain in a state of readiness for any further investigation seems to suggest the Scotland Yard did not in any way take the evidence as conclusive."

Macnaghten also identified a third suspected suspect as follows "(2) Kosminski -an Polish Jew -- & living in Whitechapel. This man went insane due to his many years of indulgence in solitude-based vices. He had a deep hatred of women, especially the prostitutes, and was a homicidal with strong tendencies: He was taken to a lunatic asylum in March 1889. There were a variety of circumstances associated to this man, which led to him being a'suspect'."

Aaron Kosminski was indeed mentally sick and was admitted to the Colney Hatch Lunatic Asylum in 1891. in contrast to Macnaghten, Anderson insisted that Kosminski was identified as the murderer, but that the man who had accused him of murder refused to stand trial against Kosminski before a the court. But, there's nothing in his asylum papers to suggest that he was violent. Instead, the asylum records show that he was suffering from hallucinations as well as fear. It is therefore unlikely that he would be capable of organizing his thoughts to the extent that the perpetrator required for him to stay hidden from detection.

Many people who have been around the issue believe that Aaron Kosminski may have been confused with Nathan Kaminsky, a bootmaker who was suffering from syphilis and was admitted to an asylum in 1888. There is a possibility that the man was identified by the asylum under the name of David Cohen, a name similar to John Doe that was typically employed to refer to Jews with names that weren't widely well-known. Cohen was frequently violent and was often confined in the asylum prior to his passed away in 1889 There is a belief that Macnaghten as well as other authorities have placed Aaron Kosminski under undue suspicion due to the incorrect spelling of Kaminsky's name.

Macnaghten's last theory of suspects was "(3) Michael Ostrog, who was a Russian doctor and convictwho was admitted to a lunatic institution as the homicidal psychopath. His ancestors were of the most egregious type, and his exact location when the killings occurred cannot be determined." But, Ostrog was a thief and a con man without a prior history of violence. However, there's also evidence to suggest that the man was actually incarcerated in an French prison during the time when the Ripper was at his most active.

Michael Ostrog

Others officers had the same suspects. There was a suspect known as Seweryn Klosowski, popularly referred to as George Chapman. Born in Poland He was moved to Whitechapel as an untrained man in the early 1888. It was later revealed that he had poisoned three of the ladies to whom he was married. acts that resulted in the execution of him in 1903.

George Chapman

A newspaper illustration depicting Chapman

In the same time frame at the time, at the same time, Pall Mall Gazette of London published two articles that accused Chapman as being the Ripper The articles were based around an interview with the Inspector Frederick Abberline. He spoke about his suspicions in detail: "I have been so amazed by the amazing connections between the two sets of murders that I've not been thinking of anything else in the days now-- not even as of the time the Attorney-General made his opening remarks during the trial of recent times, and traced the ancestors of Chapman prior to his arrival in the country in 1888. Since then, the notion has taken over my mind, and everything is woven into the picture so perfectly that I can't help but feel it's the person we have fought so hard to capture 15 years earlier. Like I said, there are many things that make it clear it is the case that Chapman is the real man, and it is important to realize that we've been unable to believe in all the myths concerning Jack the Ripper being dead or being an insane person or anything of that like that. For instance, the time of his arrival of Chapman in England is the same as that of the commencement of the murders that took place in Whitechapel There is also a correlation because the killings stopped in London after Chapman's move to America and similar crimes began to be committed in America following his arrival in America. It is also known that the fact that he was studying the field of medicine and surgery in Russia prior to coming to America is well-established and it is interesting to observe that the initial series of murders were the work of a renowned surgeon, whereas the latest poisoning cases were found to be the work of someone with more than basic understanding of medical practices. The tale told by "Chapman's wife's' about the plot to kill her with an axe while living she was in America is not something to be overlooked however there is something else that happens in America is even more fascinating."

Abberline was later asked to discuss the conversation he had with the coroner who was able to hear the case of The Whitechapel murders. Abberline explained that "The coroner ... told me that he had been informed by the curator of the museum of pathology associated to one of the major medical schools that a several months prior, an American came to him him to collect a variety of specimens. He expressed his desire to provide PS20 per specimen. Even though the curious visitor was told his request was not likely to be being fulfilled, he nevertheless urged his wish. It was later discovered it was repeated in another institution of the same nature in London. The coroner in the moment stated: 'Isn't it possible that the knowing of this demand could have prompted a wretched alcoholic to seek out one of these specimens? It is hard to believe that such inhumanity could be thought to be the case for anyone, but unfortunately, criminal records show that any criminal is indeed possible! It's an amazing fact that following the Whitechapel terrors America could have been the location where another type of murder was committed, because the criminal did not meet with the requirements for his American agent. ... It is the reality that Klosowski was a foreigner when he first came to this country was a resident of George Yard, Whitechapel Road in the area where the first murder took place is quite intriguing as is the size of the man as well as his peaked cap are reported to have worn was very tallies, in line with the descriptions I read about his appearance. The majority of people agree that Klosowski was a foreign appearance man. .... A single difference have I noticed, and it is that people who claim to have seen Jack the Ripper at some point or the other, say that he was who was between thirty and forty years old. Theyalso state that they saw only his back. It is not difficult to miss the age from a rear perspective."

Abberline made his case against Chapman with the statement, "As to the question of the difference in character in the crimes are often discussed I can't see any reason why that one person couldn't have committed both, provided that he was a professional as is evident in the case of Chapman. One who was able to watch his wife being executed through poison such as he did was capable of doing anything and it is the reason he could attempt with such brutal blooded manner , to kill his first wife using knives at the hands of his wife in New Jersey, makes one more likely to believe the idea that he was involved with the other series of murders. What could be more likely is that someone who was adept in the field of medicine and surgery would cease using knives after his commission--and I believe that Chapman received an American-issued commission -- came to an end and for the rest of his horrific deeds applied his expertise in poisons? In fact, if it can be accepted that a person who lives life on a global scale continues to practice his unforgivable practice until he is taken into custody or dies There is plenty to admire about Chapman's steadfastness. It is true that the motivation changes but the insanity isn't completely eradicated. The victims,, you'll notice, remain women, however, they belong to different classes, and clearly need different methods of killing. "Today, Chapman is mostly considered a suspect due to a variety of reasons which contrast his actions with those of Jack the Ripper. While Chapman murdered people he knew by poison, Jack the Ripper was known to stab women in the street, an utterly different approach for serial killers. Furthermore, Chapman was an immigrant and it was more unlikely that he would communicate in English to prostitutes in Whitechapel or could have been intimately acquainted with Whitechapel enough that he was able to escape the crime scene flawlessly.

In the story in the Pall Mall Gazette also introduced the name of another suspect named the Dr. Thomas Neill Cream, an abortionist who was found guilty in 1881, when he was living in America of poisoning his lover's husband. He was sentenced to 10 years in prison until his release in the year 1891 in which he resorted to another murder before being hanged in 1892. There was a claim that he did not serve his sentence, but moved places with a clone and allowed him to go back to London and take on one of the Whitechapel murders.

Cream

In the end, it's absurd to say that Cream was a credible suspect. Abberline stated that: "But what about Dr. Neill Cream? A fictitious tale is told about how he confessed to the scaffold. He was said to have gotten close to saying "I am Jack--' , but the rope's jerk ended his words. Another fictitious tale. Neill Cream was not even living in this country when the Whitechapel murders occurred. The identity of the criminal remains to be determined in spite of those who have created these stories and who claim to know the state the mind of the government."

The Pall Mall Gazette article concluded, "'You can state most in a clear and concise manner,' stated Abberline. Abberline, 'that Scotland Yard is not any wiser on this subject than it was 15 years ago. It's absurd to speak of the police being able to prove that the man has died. I have always been, and was, in most intimate contact in contact with Scotland Yard, and it was nearly impossible for me to not know all the details. In addition the fact that the authorities would be eager to see an end to this mystery, even if it was only to earn their own respect. In order to convince anyone who is unsure about the matter that he is the one to prove it, the detective. Abberline produced recent documentary evidence that put the skepticism that is Scotland Yard as to the person responsible beyond the shadow of doubt. "I'm aware," said the well-known detective that it is reported in various publications that 'Jack the Ripper was a person who was a patient in a mental asylum in the past However, there is no evidence whatsoever of a physical nature to back up this hypothesis."

According to the Pall Mall Gazette story makes evident that there were a lot of suspects who were more well-liked by reporters than among police. The most famous of these were William H. Bury. The day of Valentine's Day in 1889, the Atlanta Constitution published a story, "THE WHITECHAPEL FIEND Dundee Policemen Believe They've Caught Jack The Ripper." The article explained that "The body of a woman, hidden in a wooden chest was found Monday morning by the police in Dundee. The body was dismembered. The chest was tiny enough that the murderer was compelled by the victim's size to squeeze inside it. A husband who was the victim was arrested for suspicion of being the murderer. It was confirmed that Wm. H. Bury, the victim, killed her. Bury was an occupant in Whitechapel, London, and his ancestors' records suggest that he could be Jack the Ripper, and that he has attacks of murder mania that are unconscious. The post mortem exam conducted on the body confirmed that the woman had was strangled before being killed, and her body was later injured, her abdomen cut open, and her arms and legs were fractured and twisted. Bury claims that he left Whitechapel three weeks back. He is unable to explain the reason why he went to Whitechapel and says that he did not have any business that required his attention at Dundee. He claims that both of them were drinking heavily the night before taking a nap, and the couple do not know what prompted him to go to bed. When he awoke, he claims she was lying on the floor with a rope around her neck. The incident was triggered by a sudden and violent desire, which he can't pinpoint the cause the cause, he grabbed with a knife and began to slash the body. When his reason returned, he was scared and hurriedly stuffed the body inside the chest where it was located, hoping to flee. He discovered, however, that he was unable to remove the remains of his wife, and decided to notify the police. The theory of officers is that the wife of Bury was aware of the facts that linked him to the East end atrocities and that she accompanied Bury to Dundee to try stopping a repeat of the atrocities."

A sketch from a newspaper of Bury

Despite this that Bury was involved, the police did not

find any evidence connecting Bury in the Whitechapel

crime scene, and Bury admitted to killing his wife, that

led to his death. In his final days Bury denied any

connection to the crimes of the Ripper even though he

allegations and resulted in the press accusing a man whose name was Frederick Deeming, who had committed murder in secret, killing the wife of his former partner and their four kids in 1891. The Age reported, just following his arrest, "From the outset a suspicion of mental illness is implied and a hint to his involvement in the Whitechapel murders is hints. The body was cut and mangled as well as the method of how the cementing was done and the stealing of a house and the arduous eradication of all evidence that the incident occurred - - all these items suggest the ferocity and skill that can only be seen in the mind of a murderer who is sane regardless of how brutal as well as brutal."

Frederick Deeming

A drawing that ties Deeming in with Ripper Murders

Later, he tried to assert that he was the Ripper however, the police disqualified Deeming as a suspect, believing that he was in jail or South Africa when the murders occurred. Some people still remain convinced that Deeming wasn't in prison, and that he was leaving South Africa for England during the Ripper's murder spree which is why they believe that Deeming may be the famous killer.

In a bizarre twist in the course of things, one suspects named by the media spent the majority of his life investigating Whitechapel murders, and also blaming others. Robert Donston Stephenson was at the London Hospital shortly after the death of Mary Nicholls and watched in admiration while the doctor. Morgan Davies demonstrated to an audience the manner in which the murders could have been carried out. Stephenson reported his suspicions of the Dr. Davies to George Marsh who was an amateur detective with whom was keen to study the case, however, March, in turn, determined Stephenson to be an appealing suspect , and transferred his suspicions Scotland Yard. Scotland Yard.

The authorities swiftly disregarded Stephenson for being a possible suspect and evidence suggests that he would not leave the hospital on the time that the crime was committed. In the meantime, Stephenson continued to show an interest in the case and on December 1 1888, he sent a letter an article in his local newspaper, the Pall Mall Gazette and put his own theories: "In calmly reviewing the complete chain of events that are connected to these savage and bloodthirsty crimes the first thing that grabs the attention is that the perpetrator was gracious sufficient to (so to say) leave his card to the victim of the Mitre-square massacre. ... The card should be noted that the chalk writing (which it is believed that was written by the killer) was discovered on the wall of Mitre-square near that of the woman who was murdered. The inscription reads "The Juwes are the ones who can't be held responsible for the crime It was clearly designed to raise suspicion against the Jews. ... Juwes inspection immediately reveals that a dot was ignored by the constable who copied it, which could be the case when it was put at a distance in the same manner as foreigners. Juives therefore we place an asterisk above the third upward stroke of the word Juwes which we discover the word to be Juives meaning the French word used to describe Jews. ... Juives The person who was murdered is therefore an Frenchman."

Stephenson continued his quest to establish a motive behind these murders "There there is no doubt the killer regardless of whether he was crazy or not, has a specific motive behind his actions; However, one possible explanation of the motive has not ever been proposed. In the 19th century, with all its modernity the idea of a motive for murder would appear absurd, but it is also true that belief in superstition is hard to sustain and some of its followers do continue to use unholy rituals. ... Black magic uses the power of demons and evil spirits in place of the benevolent spirits controlled by the magicians of the haute magie.

...we uncover the link that connects modern French necromancy to the search to find the killer of the east. These substances are terrible, and they are extremely difficult to obtain. They are only available by the most horrifying crimes of which mutilation and murder of dead bodies are among the least horrific."

In a way, Stephenson's elaborate explanation only served to increase his status as a suspect to many, yet police have not found any evidence to connect Stephenson to the crime.

Robert Stephenson

Of the many suspects identified during the over 100 years after the Whitechapel murders, none are possibly as intriguing like Prince Albert Edward, the Duke of Clarence and Avondale and the son of the Prince of Wales Bertie, the daughter of Queen Victoria. Bertie. According to reports, he was "slow," and slightly deaf, he wasn't suspected of anything until more than 100 years after the incident. In the year 1962, and then in the year 1970, authors offered a variety of theories as to the reason Eddy could be the one responsible for the murder.

However, those who support this theory face a huge obstacle to overcome documents from the royal court which described every step Eddy took. The following evidence suggests it is impossible for him to have carried out the crime, as Eddy was in constant distance from London at the time of their occurrence.

"29 August to September 7th, 1888. The Prince was together with the Viscount Downe at Danby Lodge, Grosmont, Yorkshire."

"7-10 September 1888 The Prince was in his Cavalry Barracks in York."

"27-30 September The Prince was in Abergeldie,

Scotland, where the Queen Victoria noted in her journal that he had lunch with her on September 30th."

"1 November: Returned to London after a trip to York. 2-12 November The Prince was in Sandringham."

Prince Eddy
Some speculated that, even the prince wasn't the

culprit, maybe an other person from the Royal Family was involved. James Kenneth Stephen was Eddy's teacher in Cambridge and was renowned for his sexist views, even by Victorian standards. Many have also pointed out examples of his handwriting resemble that of in"From Hell" letter "From Hell" letter. There is no proof to suggest that he is the Ripper.

James Kenneth Stephen
Two other suspects belonging to The Royal Family turn up from time to time on the list of suspects. The first one are Sir John Williams, who served as the obstetrician to the youngest child of Queen Victoria Beatrice. In 2005 The book Uncle Jack, written by one of Williams his descendants, stated that the doctor

murdered the women and cut them into pieces to find out more about infertility. His spouse, Lizzie, had been infertile. However, there was no evidence to establish a connection between Williams with the deaths and there was no evidence to connect Lizzie herself with the killings, and she has been blamed by some of the murders.

Williams

Another suspect associated with those of the Victorian courts was sir William Gull, who served as a physician for the Queen herself. The report suggests that he may have been assisted in the crime through John Netley, his coachman However, There isn't any evidence to link either of them to the crime.

A number of well-known people in recent times is James Maybrick, who had been thought to be the creator of a diary where the author said he was Jack the Ripper. The diary was first published in the early 1990s through Michael Barrett, who later admitted that it was a fake and, at that point, the scam was so well-known that Barrett was having a difficult time stopping the ruse. On January 15, 1995 Barrett wrote, "Since December 1993, I've been trying through the media and the Publishers and the Author of the Book, Mrs Harrison as well as my Agent Doreen Montgomery to discredit the fraudulent nature of "The diary of Jack the Ripper ' ('the diary'). No one will believe me, and, in actual fact, some highly influential individuals within the Publishing and Film world have done everything they can to defame me, and in fact, they've gone as that they have introduced an entirely new story of the true facts of the diary and how it was discovered. The facts are as follows: I Michael Barratt (sic) was the creator of the original diary of Jack the Ripper'. My partner, Anne Barrett, hand recorded it using my notes that I typed as well as at times at my dictate, the specifics of which I'll explain in due time. The concept of the Diary originated from a conversation among Tony Devereux, Anne Barrett my wife and I at a time that I thought an elaborate hoax was a real possibility. We delved into his background James Maybrick and I read everything related to his involvement in the Jack the Ripper matter. I believed that James Maybrick was the perfect person to be a potential candidate to play Jack the Ripper. But, most importantly, Maybrick was unable to defend himself. He wasn't 'Jack the Ripper' of that I'm sure but, the dates, locations, trips to London and all that matched. It was (sic) be easy (sic). I informed my wife Anne Barrett I told her"Anne, I'll write an best-selling book this time, we're guaranteed to succeed'. When I realized that we could achieve it. We would need to gather the required materials, including pen, paper, and ink. I thought about this seriously. Around the time of January and February of 1990, Anne Barrett and I finally decided to record"The Diary of Jack the Ripper."

Florence as well as James Maybrick

In spite of the confession, and other similar confessions, many believe that Maybrick wasn't just Jack the Ripper however, the same sequence of killings within the United States, even as the latest research has proved that the diary was in fact fake.

Chapter 6: Prime Suspects

"I think it's the stuff of legends. ."--An unnamed Ripperologist Criminals, the best crime is the one that is not solved. It's obvious enough.

But could this cold case be the ideal case for certain sleuths who are who are on the opposite side of the hunt?

The not solved crime is the most famous one ever recorded in the history of mankind There are thousands of cold trail to trace for any of the hundreds of possible suspects and real suspects. If it's about Jack the Ripper, there's no end to the terror or fascination that drives individuals of different backgrounds to investigate the subject and wrestle with the clues that countless others have tried to solve.

Law enforcement and serious academic experts have been studying the case since the killing started. The same is true for historians, journalists as well as novelists, detectives in armchairs and conspiracy theorists, as well as criminalologists, scientists, FBI profilers, movie producers, tour guides and many other people.

Many of the hobbies that we enjoy today have been born from studying and have led to life-long jobs. If you find yourself or himself among the millions who find the criminal mind to be endlessly fascinating It's the endless pool of theories, clues, possibilities and dead ends which make the Jack the Ripper investigation an "perfect" case.

Some of the Ripperologists as well as professionals and amateurs alike The case remains a mystery that's unlikely to be solved. Others believe that they've solved the mystery, placing the murders on one of the individuals London police were focused on in the past, however, they never brought charges or charged with any other probable or suspects that are wildly unlikely.

More than one hundred men and a few women have been identified in the process and it is likely that there will be many more people of interest who will be discovered in the time to come.

There are so many unanswered questions concerning the investigation and the suspects, anyone who was close to London during the summer and into the early autumn of 1888 could be suspected of being involved. Many were.

Is Jack the Ripper an ophthalmologist with a surgical background? A meat cutter, butcher or maybe somebody who worked at morgue? A woman who was trained in midwifery? An "moral crusader" who is aiming a hammer at evil? Someone who is aiming to bring an end to immigrants?

How did the saga commence and then end abruptly? Did the Ripper be imprisoned for a different offense, or perhaps in a mental institution? Did he escape and go on to commit murder in another location, possibly it was the U.S. or Australia, according to some theories? Did he die? Did he simply disappear into a routine daily routine that is typical of his?

Time has demonstrated that there are a myriad of ways to put the pieces together, however to date there are no conclusive theories. Every time a theory is presented there are those who challenge it as strongly.

Yet, even after many years, a few suspects have made it into the spotlight or were there from the beginning, and Ripperologists have reached a as if they are the most likely suspects.

Seweryn Antonowicz Klosowski (George Chapman)
Seweryn Antonowicz Klosowski was among the prime suspects, according to certain investigators at the scene, particularly the Chief Inspector Frederick Abberline of the London Metropolitan Police.

Abberline was seen as to be one of the key characters in the investigation due to the fact that he was acquainted with the Whitechapel district very well and had worked there in various capacities over the years during his rise up the ranks.

Klosowski was born in Poland in 1865. He relocated in Poland in 1865. He emigrated to the United Kingdom sometime in 1887 or 1888, just before the Ripper came to the scene. He resided in Whitechapel and was employed as a barber at the time the canonical murders took place and was known as Ludwig Schloski. It was believed and documented in a number of books as well as in the Pall Mall Gazette, that

Klosowski was the most wanted Inspector Abberline's suspect during the investigation. As with any suspect, the authorities were unable to prove an argument against the suspect.

However, time did show the fact that Klosowski (who switched his identity as George Chapman five or six years after the murders) was a rotten apple, as like Abberline believed. In the end, he was found guilty of murdering each of his three wives each one using poison, and was executed in 1903.

It is true that the fact that Jack turned out to be an acknowledged killer, however it did not end up making it more clear that he was Jack the Ripper, though it did give him an alternative name: "the Borough Poisoner." It was more of a way to discredit the theory since serial killers typically choose their M.O. and then stick to the same one, as critics of the theory of Abberline pointed out. Over a century later, Klosowski/Chapman still remains in the list of possible suspects.

Aaron Kosminski

Another Polish immigrants, Aaron Kosminski (or Kozminski) is identified as being a definite suspect by the top police officers. The late Sir Melville Macnaghten named Kosminski as one of three main suspects in a memorandum from 1894 concerning the investigation. The Chief Inspector Donald Swanson wrote a long-lost note that referred to Kosminski as a character in his memoirs written by another key character in the case assistant commissioner Sir Robert Anderson. In his own words, Anderson referred to Kosminski only lightly in his book but did not mention him directly.

Macnaghten did actually favor one or three of them as the murderer, but did not exclude Kosminski. Swanson did however point his finger directly at Kosminski in the notes he made on the pages of his version Anderson's book. The interesting thing was that these notes weren't brought to surface until 1987, after which one of Swanson's heirs made the notes public. Anderson wrote that an eyewitness got close-up views of the murderer, and had identified the suspect "the moment he came into contact by him" however, he refused to be a witness. Swanson clarified this in his annotation in pencil and wrote "Kosminski was the suspected suspect" and then inscribing "DSS."

The witness was not willing to testify, citing that both him and the suspect both were Jews, Anderson, said that he did not want to be the one to blame for the execution which was certain to follow the conviction of the killer. But the suspect was aware that he had been exposed and was monitored around all hours by police, and he halted his rampage of murder.

Kosminski born in 1865 was born in 1865, was a Polish Jew who was admitted to a mental hospital in 1891. He was in the asylum until his demise in 1919. The idea that Jack the Ripper has strong supporters and detractors who are fervent However, all attempts to verify it using the latest techniques (including an analysis using DNA which didn't yield conclusive results) have failed.

FBI profiler John Douglas weighed what is known about Kosminski's mental health against what's known about the psychological issues faced by serial killers, but couldn't find any correlation in as well.

Montague John Druitt

Of the suspects mentioned by Sir Melville Mcnaghten's memoandum Macnaghten himself believed Montague John Druitt as the top contender, though he used inaccurate information, at most partially, to arrive at the conclusion.

Druitt was born in 1857. He was a barrister -a lawyer who also served as assistant schoolmaster. He was abruptly removed from the post of schoolmaster in the latter part of 1888. He was found dead shortly afterwards. His death took place shortly following his murder Mary Jane Kelly, the last canonical victim on the 9th of November. The body of his decomposing corpse was discovered lying in the Thames on the 31st of December 1888.

His timing for his death was a draw for a possible suspect for Macnaghten.

The man also claimed that he had twenty many years later after the killings, to possess "private data" from well-known sources. After he left the police force in 1913 Macnaghten claimed to journalists the media that he "knew the precise name that was Jack the

Ripper," but he would not reveal it.

These sources came to light in the public domain only some years in the past. It is believed that an Tory politician, H.R. Farquharson who lived close to Druitt and was an intimate friend of Macnaghten's, who was also associated with Macnaghten's family, the Druitt family, was a suspect in the presence of the Police Chief.

However, there's an abundance of experts willing to challenge the theory, which is the case with almost all theories in the matter. One reason is that they claim that Macnaghten put too excessive importance on Druitt's death in his connection with Jack the Ripper. Certain Ripperologists claim that he could be homosexual, which is one of the reasons the school fired him . It was also a source for shame as well as a crime that was punishable with imprisonment in the time. They also point out that there was an underlying mental illness within the immediate Druitt family. Some point out the obvious facts that Macnaghten's written works concerning Druitt which include the fact that he identified him as a doctor , and ignoring the possibility of an alibi to at least one murder.

Joseph Barnett

Mary Jane Kelly's friend Joseph Barnett did not rise to the top of the suspect list until the 1970s. However, Barnett has been a serious candidate since.

According to the theory formulated by a variety of reputable researchers it boils down to that: Barnett was deeply in love with Mary Jane Kelly, Jack the Ripper's final victim and was deeply disturbed by the fact by the fact that she had reverted to prostitutes after losing his job just prior to the Ripper murders began. Although the couple continued to meet regularly, Barnett left the room they shared--the same room in which she later died--when Kelly permitted other prostitutes to remain in the room, while Kelly continued to perform sexual activity.

Barnett was furious at Mary Jane's actions and, most likely, a result of his inability to stand by Mary Jane's decision. To keep her from his streets, he devised an elaborate plan to kill all the women. But in the end the plot was unsuccessful, and he realized that she didn't feel the same way about him as the other women did. On the 9th of November the killer took revenge by slapping her with the kind of rage that criminal experts have discovered suggests that the killer and the victim shared a close bond.

The argument goes far over and above that, too. Thirty years old five feet seven inches tall and sporting a mustache moderate size, blue eyes and fair skin, Barnett was a good description of the witnesses police needed to compare against. The theory can explain the simple chatter as well as the laughing George Hutchinson observed between the two men as they walked towards the home. Barnett acting as the Mary Jane Kelly's murderer also addressed the question of why her body was discovered locked in her room. The killer was the owner of keys. Barnett who lived in the room along with Kelly for a brief period prior to the attack, was able to leave and return without difficulty. In the end, if Barnett had been Jack the Ripper, he could not continue to murder after Mary Jane's murder, which is why the murders came to an end with her death.

From the perspective in the last decade of the twentieth century, with the aid of modern profiling technology, Barnett was a perfect match to the likely killer identified in the FBI analysis.

The FBI profile of the killer would exhibit these characteristics:

It was an white male between the ages of 28 and 36 and working or living within Whitechapel.

Whitechapel area.

He was raised by an abusive or absent father in his early years.

The perpetrator likely had a job that allowed him to legally

Feel the destructive tendencies of his.

Jack the Ripper probably ceased his murder because it was either a case of another offense, or felt near to being identified as the perpetrator.

The perpetrator was likely to have an issue with his physical structure which caused an abundance of anger or frustration.

And how does Joseph Barnett fit the criteria?

Barnett was aged 30 white, and lived within 1 mile of

Whitechapel for the rest of his life.
Joseph's father passed away at the age of six.
Barnett was employed as a fish keeper, and had experience in
Boning and gutting the bones and gutting.
Barnett was interrogated by the police for four hours following the Kelly murder The police were pleased with his testimonies.
Barnett might have suffered from an impairment in speech called echolalia (the involuntary repetition of another's words) According to news accounts of the evidence he gave at the inquiry.
Of course, as with everything Ripper there are people who are on both sides of the argument The theory appears to be a solid one and has gained momentum over the last four decades.

David Cohen

In the heavily immigrant Whitechapel area, David Cohen emerged as an additional suspect, who is identified as "Leather Apron" by at least one reputable Ripperologist. After the initial canonical Ripper murders, in which outrage and shock fueled an anti-immigrant, anti-Semitic fury A third man named John Pizer was taken into custody and was briefly held as a possible suspect according to earlier.

In a book published in 1987, Ripperologist Martin Fido proposed another Polish Jew as a suspect: David Cohen, as the authorities knew him as a violent, antisocial man who was admitted to Colney Hatch

Lunatic Asylum shortly after the murders were stopped and died there in the year following. In the asylum, Cohen was deemed by the authorities to be violent, and even destructive. However, he wasn't "David Cohen."

Fido said that the name was commonly used in England similarly to the way we employ John Doe as a generic name, but its use was less narrow since it specifically targeted an Jewish immigrants who was unidentified or whose identity was too complex. Fido believed that the authorities investigating The Jack the Ripper investigation had misunderstood with the name Kosminski and Kaminsky and that the confusion led police to believe they were looking at the wrong person. The attention, Fido suggested, belonged to Aaron Kaminski, a bootmaker who was previously treated for syphilis instead of Kosminski.

Kaminsky was a resident of Whitechapel however, after his death in 1888 or just before when the killings occurred, his exact location were not clear. Kaminsky could have vanished in the Jack the Ripper rampage and ended up in the asylumas David Cohen shortly after the rampage ended. The concept has been supported by John Douglas, the FBI profiler, who stated in his book of 1989 that the available behavioral clues indicated that the man was "known by the authorities by the name of David Cohen... or someone similar to his."

Prince Albert Victor

Of all those who have been suspects of involvement in the Ripper murders in one way or some other time One of the most well-known and persistent could be Prince Albert, the grandson of Queen Victoria and the son of the king Edward VII and Princess Alexandra. Prince Albert Victor, known to his family and friends as Eddy was born 1864 and was widely considered to be loved but a bit backward, dependent on school tutors and apathetic, deaf or perhaps mentally unstable and having an IQ that was low. IQ.

However, one thing he was not thought of as one of the suspects for the Ripper's Whitechapel murders -- not in his entire life in any way. Perhaps surprisingly, but perhaps in the end, he has been the main focus of many speculations developed around the investigation. Similar to many others that are connected to the crime and the murders, he was only made suspected after his death, however certain theories that have been proposed from the 1960s onwards are all the intrigue in the palace of any Shakespearean drama.

The most complicated situations involve Freemasons as well as cooperation with police, as well as different relatives of the royal family such as the Queen Victoria herself.

According to one story the story goes that the women were executed due to the fact they were killed because the prince, second next in the line for the throne was secretly married and been fathered by a

Catholic commoner.

In another instance, Prince Eddy was exacting revenge after contracting a venereal infection caused by a prostitute. Or that he was suffering from the venereal disease which affected his brain, causing him to go into homicidal psychosis The idea was formulated in a book published in 1970 by an British doctor, who claimed that the other Royals were aware of what was going on in the moment.

Since the theory first came up and subsequently proven to be true, it has been mentioned numerous instances and taken many varieties, from a novel detailing a palace plot From Hell, a 2001 Johnny Depp movie that implicated Eddy.

Many experts have ruled out the notion that Eddy was involved in the murders in any way or through the use of substitutes or taking matters to his own. They also claimed they had no proof that the prince had any venereal disease. If anyone is unsure if the validity of the theory one only has examine news articles published in the early months of 2016 where two separate letters written by Eddy to his doctor, confirming that he, actually, suffer from an infection called gonorrhea.

It could lend some credence to one aspect to the tale, however it didn't address larger issues as one expert on crime observed in the Guardian newspaper's article that announced the letters were going to be auctioned off. One thing is that Prince Albert Victor

didn't come near to matching the description police used to describe him. In addition, the prince was believed to be located in Scotland during when one of those murders.
"I think it's an untruth," he told the reporter.

Chapter 7: The Art of Murder

"I swear I did not strike with the very first punch ."--Francis Thompson

The mystery may have been solved when James Maybrick's diary in the year 1992 or even with its publication in the year that followed. Maybrick is a successful cotton merchant , and an associate with Jack the Ripper, but his name was never mentioned as a suspect in the investigation until that book was discovered one hundred years later. Before that the time Maybrick was involved in the killing in the past, it was because the wife of his victim had murdered him using arsenic.

Like most things related to the Ripper, the Victorian scrapbook, which was actually an extensive confession to the murders of 1888 prompted more questions than it provided. First, the diary did not contain Maybrick's name, but it was inscribed "Jack Ripper" Ripper"--although it's true that there's sufficient personal details in it that a person could believe it was written by him. In addition, Ripperologists were skeptical of the authenticity of the diary, pointing at contradictory and incorrect passages, and a majority considered the whole thing to be an untruth.

The diary, which had the first 20 pages removed it was discovered through Michael Barrett, an unemployed scrap metal dealer from Liverpool. Barrett offered at least a several different versions of its origins throughout the following years. In one the tale is that a friend offered the item to him at an establishment. In another version, it had been owned by his wife for a long time.

A few years later, after the initial discovery the man swore, in affidavits two times, that he was "the creator of the manuscript composed by my wife, Anne Barrett, at my transcription, known by the name of The Jack the Ripper Diary." This wasn't the final word in the debate, however; the witness later retracted his testimony.

All through, the majority of Ripperologists have remained skeptical and it's safe to say that the majority of them still do. However, several rounds tests by scientists have complicated the question. Many scientists performed experiments on ink to see whether the chemicals present in it were those used in Victorian inks however, different tests produced various, contradictory outcomes. However, those who believe that the diary is authentic claim that the tests established its origins in the nineteenth century and that only police and the killer would be aware of some of the details contained in the diary.

The two camps each have advocates Of course however the diary is also an significant piece of another theory formulated by screenwriter and film director Bruce Robinson, who spent 15 years studying the Ripper case in his book of the same name in 2015. Love Jack. James Maybrick, Robinson concluded was not Jack the Ripper after all. The murderer in fact was

Michael Maybrick, his younger brother. Michael Maybrick, a well-known songwriter and singer. Robinson's theory is fascinating in its own right, but so does the reality that this cult musician isn't only a renowned member of the world of art to make it onto those list of possible suspects. It's interesting that, in Robinson's book Michael Maybrick joins a roster of artists that includes a well-known poet, a renowned painter, a well-known actor as well as one of the pioneers of detective stories and, of course the creator of one of the most popular books for children that are published in English.

A Star Singer-Songwriter is an Unknown Suspect Michael Maybrick, or as his name was more popularly known, "Stephen Adams," was a well-known name during his time. A well-known musician who was classically educated in organ, piano and vocals. He had the fame both in Italy as well as England as a baritone. In the 1870s, was also a composer whose works were the first to be recorded.

composed under the pseudonym "James, "achieved extraordinary popularity." One of the songs, an ocean song dubbed "Nancy Lee,"" sold over 100,000 sheets of music which made it a kind of Top 40 hit in its day. The other compositions varied from sentimental and romantic to religious in their subject and tones.

One of his sacred tunes, "The Holy City," can still be heard and recorded to this day. Another one, the well-known "They all love Jack" was a ominous reference to the notorious killer to some people.

He was frequently regarded as an equal to his fellow composers Gilbert and Sullivan When the time came to pass, an obituary author wrote:

The moment the news came across on the internet the news that Michael Maybrick, or 'Stephen Adams as he was than many of us, had passed away longer with us, a deep sense of loss to a loved one was created that only the passing of only a handful of men could provoke. Anyone within the British Isles hasn't been captivated by the beautiful music of his numerous songs that are all pure and inspiring with some of the most grand and devotionally stimulating in the depths of their religious conviction.

But he was also more than a renowned artist and composer Robinson insists in his meticulously researched and thoroughly documented 800-page book. The man is Jack the Ripper, and the symbol for serial killers, with an intense hatred for women and an "sociopathological" personality as well as a huge self-esteem, Robinson wrote.

He argues his case with numerous documents that includes letters, railroad timetables , among others that place the travelling entertainer in the scene of the canonical murders and numerous other locations of murder throughout the United States, arguing that Jack the Ripper was responsible for numerous victims that have not been previously acknowledged.

Robinson added that it wasn't due to the high quality

of the police's work in the case that enabled Maybrick to escape his crimes, but an organized conspiracy that involved his colleagues Freemasons and high-ranking officials in the police force and even government officials in the mix, he said that in an up-to date version of the old theory.

DNA Evidence at the Last Patricia Cornwell, the famous mystery writer whose bestsellers are based on the latest scientific research, has settled on another suspect, which was an artist instead of an artist.
To arrive at that result, Cornwell applied modern research to documents that are found in the Ripper case files, and reported the findings within her 2002 publication that she confidently named Portrait of a Killer: Jack the Ripper--Case closed. Cornwell recruited a team of forensic scientists to look over documents that might be connected to Jack (the famous "Dear Boss" letter, among other documents) to determine mitochondrial DNA. The DNA was then compared with mitochondrial DNA that was found in documents written by famous English painter Walter Sickert.
The team of forensic scientists led by Cornwell discovered a mitochondrial DNA (mtDNA) in a number of Ripper letters that were matched to sequences that were found on a number of documents written by Sickert. Watermarks with specific watermarks were also found to Sickert's letter and those addressed to media and the police. If these results are correct

According to Cornwell, Walter Sickert was Jack the Ripper.

The painter and printmaker born in Germany was a printmaker and painter who relocated from Germany to England together with family when he was an infant and spent his first years studying art at one of Britain's most prestigious academies, before dropping out of school in his late teens to attend classes with and be an associate of the famous artist James Abbott McNeill Whistler. In the following years Sickert met Edgar Degas while visiting Paris and was influenced by an influence from the school of Impressionism. As an artist who was maturing, Sickert gained considerable prominence as an advocate of avant-garde ideas as an intermediary between Impressionism and Modernism and had a significant impression on British art until the 20th century.

He was also believed for having a lot of attention to his research into the Jack the Ripper investigation, and believed that he resided in the same room Jack was in and based on a story the landlady shared. His work covered the vast array of topics throughout his long career (he was alive until 1942). The majority of his paintings were of theatre as well as music hall sceneries, inside scenes photographs, and naked figures (Winston Churchill being one example). He was also noted for painting images of a series centered around a particular theme. A well-known series was based off the "Camden Town Murder" the murder of a prostitute murdered in 1907, her throat cut off on her bed.

For some, the works of the series prove that Sickert was fascinated with sexual violence. the artist was able to make it onto the roster of Ripper suspects prior to when Cornwell did ever take up the case. The book by Cornwell was the third in the modern era to blame Walter Sickert. In a 1976 book, he was tagged as a participant in another conspiracy that also involved Freemasons and Royals as well as a 1990 book declared that he was an actual Ripper himself. The evidence provided by Cornwell ranged from DNA evidence, to watermarks discovered on letters to a notion--apparently unproven Sickert was suffering from the "congenital anomaly in the penis" which rendered him ineffective and caused him to become angry at women. There are other accounts that claim the womanizer was the father of several illegitimate children.

The evidence from science has been viewed with suspicion by a lot of researchers. There may be a connection between Sickert and a few of the Ripper correspondence, however it's up for debate. The tests on DNA could reveal that Sickert and someone else who dealt with the letters had certain genetic characteristics however it is not able to demonstrate that those traits were connected to a specific person. Anything from one to 10 percent of the population could be a good candidate according to some researchers. In addition the majority, if not all instances of Ripper letters were probably hoaxes. Even if they could connect Sickert to a few with absolute certainty, it could just prove that he was among hoaxers.

There is nothing conclusive.

The Poet was Motivated by an Motive

If it wasn't the artist, perhaps that was the poet. Not only did renown English poet Francis Thompson write poems and

Stories of killing prostitutes both prior to and following Jack's murder rampage, he studied medicine for six years in which time he probably acquired a wealth of knowledge dissecting corpses. Also, he was an opium user who lived a poverty-stricken life in Whitechapel prior to being discovered among the elite literary community and his only relationship was with a prostitute who lived there that broke up with him. The ending of the relationship and the subsequent addiction to drugs and other causes led him to the edge and made him into a terrifying killer according to speculation that his darkest writings hint at a brutal double life.

"I swear I didn't strike the first strike. The force of my hand seized it and pushed the poniard to the ground. Then she began crying; and me, in a state of rage and dreading detection, dreading most of all her awakening, I struck again and again she cried, and repeatedly, and again she cried." He said in his 1889 tale which some believe to be an indication of the meaning he inserted into his work (a Poniard was a tiny dagger).

In reality, it happened to Richard Patterson, an English instructor and author who lives in Australia who turned his attention on Thompson in a book published in 2015. Patterson experienced his breakthrough in 1997, when he was still studying at. The young man was struck with the fusion of the poet's often gruesome writing, his experience to become a doctor his use of drugs and the gruelling life in street corners of Whitechapel just prior to the time he rose to the top of the heap. Patterson was also known carrying the dissecting knife in his coat whenever walking in the rough neighborhoods and had his weapon of murder always in his pocket. Patterson's work was published as the form of a brief book in 1998. He followed it up with the work was expanded in 2015. It was during the time that Thompson resided with his prostitute love that his talents were recognized and he earned the patrons that led to his success. However, that haphazard event also had darker ramifications, Patterson believed. Because she believed that they would make him look unpopular with public opinion and literary circles, if they were to learn about his affair to her, she decided to end her relationship, causing him experience an emotional breakdown. Broken down or not, Thompson was able to achieve immense success as a writer and was respected by the next generation of writers following his early death at the age of 47. Literature legends like J.R.R. Tolkien For instance claimed that Thompson's work had influential on him and also the novelist Madeleine L'Engle used a line from Thompson's poem "The Mistress of Vision" to name her novel Troubling a Star.

The Actor Who portrayed Pure Evil

There was also the actor who didn't need to wait a hundred years before suspicion would be thrown at his shoulders. While Jack was in the middle of London there were people in awe of Richard Mansfield, an American actor in the London stage in a stage production that was based on Robert Lewis Stevenson's Dr. Jekyll and Mr. Hyde. The transformation of Mansfield on stage from evil to good appeared so convincing, and disturbing that the audience began to believe it was a reflection of the real world.

He began the show just prior to when the Ripper began to kill the victims, and in early October the suspicions that had been whispered were confirmed after they City of London Police received the letter, which spoke out about the concerns the play caused. The play was plagued by spelling and grammar mistakes The letter read in particular:

What I'm going to say seems almost impossible however, strange events have occurred occasionally. I have a great love of actors. I'm not the only one to think that because a man is a part that is dretful and that is why he is bad, But when I saw Mr Mansfield Take the Part of Dr Jekel and Mr Hyde I felt at time that he was what the one I wanted to be and I've been unable to let this thought out of my head. ....

The writer continued to mention that the murders took place in the evenings in the evenings when Mansfield was not in the office (at that time, the two first of the Ripper's most famous victims had passed away, the third only a few days earlier). The writer also stated that newspapers reported similar murders were committed in America and in the United States, which was where Mansfield typically resided and worked in the same place, and that the perpetrator was never caught. The letter was addressed as "One who prays for the Murderer to get Caught." This reports shook Mansfield as an actor, and also at the theatre. To try and regain the trust of the public, Mansfield offered to perform an act, this time a comedy, to aid a social reform group that was raising funds to set up a laundry in order to create jobs for prostitutes who had been treated to rehabilitation. The show was eventually cancelled after the negative publicity made him leave the London stage in the midst of.

The bad press never ended in any way. In the event of his death nearly a years after his death, the obituary published was published in The New York Times remembered Mansfield as "the best actor of his time and among the most outstanding of all time." The praise was hidden under a stack of headlines, which read "Richard Mansfield, one-time Ripper suspect, died 1907/ Started Jekyll and Hyde on the stage of The Lyceum August 1888." In the present his name is sure to appear on any list of famous suspects.

The Case For Sherlock Holmes?

Sometimes the Sir Arthur Conan Doyle is named as a suspect in addition however there's no evidence to suggest that many people will take the suggestion seriously. When the crime was committed the author was only 3 years old and was pursuing a medical profession and had begun writing short stories to earn a living.

The majority of his accusers have concentrated on his medical background and knowledge that of the criminal brain as shown in the stories of Sherlock Holmes. Sherlock Holmes, to link his involvement with Jack the Ripper. Some have claimed without providing evidence that during his 1887 time as a surgeon for ship on whaling vessels and that he took "sadistic pleasure" when he killed the animals. This is about all the evidence against him , though at least one of the writers has decided to argue that he resolved the crimes, not the ones he committed.

In this scenario, Conan Doyle and Dr. Joseph Bell, his real-life sleuthing mentor were believed to have known the identity of the murderer. They kept the information secret because they were aware that Jack The Ripper was not actually Prince Albert Victor, as some believed, but rather his personal mentor, James K. Stephen. They decided not to make the news public about their discovery since it could cause disgrace on their Royal family, as the story is told.

A Suspect in Wonderland

Every look to find Jack the Ripper appears to lead it's way to another famous artist from Victorian England. In this instance we have a suspect in Lewis Carroll, the children's author who invented the worlds of fantasy that were immortalized by Alice's Adventures in Wonderland and other works. The author has been considered a possibility since the the author Richard Wallace tied not only Carroll (whose real name was Charles Dodgson) but also his co-author, Thomas Vere Bayne, to the murders in his book from 1996.

Carroll, Wallace said, admitted to the crimes by putting clever anagrams -- words or phrases that were created by rearranging letters of an additional word or phrase throughout Alice's Adventures in Wonderland and another book, both released within the year that followed the murder of the Ripper. Alongside the word games Wallace claimed to have seen numbers in the text and speculated about the possibility of connections between Carroll, Bayne, and Montague Druitt, the more common suspect previously discussed.

In scouring Carroll's works and rearranging the text Wallace discovered evidence of this kind and in the beginning paragraphs of his book he stated the following:

This is my tale about Jack the Ripper, the man who was the source of Britain's most notorious unsolved murders. The story leads to the most unlikely of suspects one who wrote tales for children. The man in question was Charles Dodgson, better known as Lewis Carroll, author of popular books such as Alice in Wonderland.

Wallace's critics, on other hand, noted the fact that Carroll and Bayne were able to provide plausible alibis for some of the murders and that there was no evidence of connection to one of them. They also pointed out that it's possible to delve into every long piece of text to discover hidden codes, regardless of whether they really exist or not. To demonstrate this certain individuals have taken advantage of Wallace and have identified "secret anagrams" in Wallace's work.

In this spirit two experts on anagrams were identified as Francis Heaney and Guy Jacobson changed the opening paragraphs of Wallace's novel upside down and rearranged the words from the first passage in a humorous new form they published on Ripperology and online bookstores:

The truth is that The truth is that I Richard Wallace, stabbed and killed a mute Nicole Brown in cold blood by severing her throat using my trusted strokes of a shiv. I was the one who set up the name of Orenthal James Simpson. He is completely innocent of the murder. P.S. The sonnets I composed were Shakespeare's as well as a few of the works of Francis Bacon too.

However, in certain ways, there could be a strong link to Lewis Carroll and Jack the Ripper. Anyone who is determined to find Jack the Ripper after all the years could be traveling, like Lewis Carroll's Alice did down an alleyway or through a look-through to a dream world where everything isn't the way it seems.

Chapter 8: The Jack the Ripper Complex

"People during that time were suffering from what could be described by some as"the Jack the Ripper complex. When a murder or mauling was discovered either in Whitechapel or in another area of the country, they came into the conclusion that Jack the Ripper was the perpetrator. In other areas of the country there was always the nagging belief that one day or another Jack the Ripper would leave Whitechapel and return to the area in which they lived. Police were not confused by alarms from other areas. In Whitechapel our investigations continued and on. The police chiefs of Scotland Yard continued to make their headquarters at Leman Street Police Station, struggling with their problems for hours after the public was convinced that all chances of catching the thief had been lost. One of the most significant conclusions that could be drawn from the incident was that the person that we were looking for was sexually obsessed. This particular angle of investigation was pursued tirelessly. Investigations were conducted at asylums throughout the United States including Broadmoor, which was the Criminal Lunatic Asylum at Broadmoor in the hope of determining if a homicidal lunatic had been released and healed around the time that the Ripper crime spree began. The investigation failed to uncover any evidence that could be useful. The anonymous letters and postcards continue to arrive increasing our investigation without providing one important clue." Walter Dew Walter Dew

From the beginning, police had to be cautious when giving anyone special attention. Walter Drew recalled "As may be imagined, hatred for the Ripper was high. The mood of the populace was so fierce that, had police had the good luck to detain him in a public area and they were luckyindeed to transport him to an police station. A number of innocent people barely escaped being lynched at the anger of a crowd."

He also described an unjustly-conducted incident that illustrates how desperate the situation was. "One one of those suspects around this particular incident was a man who was locally known in the area as "Leather Apron". He was not a well-known character that was well-known in the eyes of the law enforcement. In addition, he always had boots with rubber soles that matched the popular notion of the quiet-working Ripper. Leather Apron was a small heavy-built, muscular man of Jewish appearance. He was a popular name locally due to the fact that he was always wearing an apron of small leather. Following his murder, Martha Turner murder, 'Leather Apron ' vanished from his usual places of residence. The streets he was rummaging through in the evenings stopped. There followed the Mary Nicholls' tragedy, and in their desire to find someone who would meet the criteria, all of the residents of the East End seemed to jump simultaneously and conclude that the man police were able to identify was actually 'Leather Apron'. "Get 'Leather Apron'" became the common cry. 'Lynch him!'"

Dew pointed out the absurdity of the scenario by noting that if authorities ever did manage to catch Jack the Ripper the Ripper, they'd need to safeguard the public from him as a part of their job: "It became necessary for the police to search for "Leather Apron" if only to safeguard him from the consequences which he would likely endure if he were to fall into the arms members of the mob. The man's description was then circulated. The man was then being located. He was spotted by a police officer who was hiding inside a residence located in Mulberry Street, and in order to not draw attention on the streets, the two walked in a normal manner towards Leman Street Police-Station. "Leather Apron liked the caring of the officer who stumbled upon him. He was not deluded about the danger that was threatening him. He was in hiding, not from police and the media, but from the general public. It's amazing how quickly the news about this type of incident goes around. "Leather Apron wasn't locked and keyed for more than an hour before hundreds stood outside the police station shouting to take him down. There was a general celebration. The Terror was now in the past! The terror was no longer a threat. The people thought so. They were not right. "Leather Apron" made an accounting of his actions over the past 10 days. The statement was if true, would rule the possibility of him being a as the murderer Mary Nicholls. Each and every detail of the statement was thoroughly scrutinized. It was determined to be true. If it was normal, the man was immediately released. The police were not against him back then. But, given how the public was being in a mood it would have been the murder of a innocent man. Therefore "Leather Apron was kept safe until an inquest was reopened on Mrs. Nicholls at which his name was cleared of any public controversy. Then he was released, and to the best of my can tell, was never abused. Then, it was shortly after that the call to 'Leather Apron' was given its place to the cry of Jack the Ripper.."

In the same way when news broke about the murders, police received a flood of correspondence from those claiming that they were the ones who committed the crime. While the majority of these were found to be ineligible for any attention, a handful were thought to be of interest and may have been were written possibly by Jack Ripper himself. Ripper himself. For instance, the Dear Boss letter, which did not just help in the creation of Jack the Ripper's term Jack Ripper, but also helped coin the name Jack Ripper but also appeared to foretell the loss of the next murderer's ear was one of the most well-known following the deaths of Elizabeth Stride and Catherine Eddowes. Detective Inspector Edmund Reid was called upon to collect preliminary evidence regarding the murder of Elizabeth Stride. He said, "A thorough search was carried out by the police in the area and the homes within however there was no trace of anyone suspected to have been responsible for the crime. After the search was complete, the entire group of people who entered the yard, as well as people who were members of the society were questioned with their addresses and names taken and the police searched their purses authorities, their clothing as well as their hands examined by doctors. The suspects were 28 in total. Each one was handled individually, and they were recorded their own names. The homes were examined twice, with the owners were examined, and their rooms were searched. A nearby loft was searched but no sign was identified of the person who was murdered. A sketch was made of the body and was it was circulated via wires around the stations. Investigations were conducted at various houses along that street. But no one was found to have experienced a disturbance or screams in the night. I looked at the wall the place where the body was found however, I could not find any areas of blood. Around half-past four, the body was taken into the morgue. After revealing the details of what happened to the body to the coroner, I returned to the yard for another check and discovered the blood had been wiped away. As it was daylight, I scoured the walls with great care and could not find any indications of being sanded."

Edmund Reid
Constable Henry Lamb soon arrived at the scene, and later testified to what he observed there while attempting to fill with as much detail as he could while

at the same time trying to protect the public from the most grotesque facts: "I sent the other constable to the nearest doctor, and the young man waiting by was taken into the station to tell the inspector about what had happened. At the time of my arrival, there were about 30 people in the yard and I was followed by others. Nobody was closer than a meter from the body. When I began to examine the deceased , the mourners began to gather and I pleaded with the crowd to stay away in case they got their clothes stained by blood and therefore be in trouble. I put my hands over the cheek. ... Then I felt my wrist however, I could not detect any pulse movements. I then whistled to assist. Her left leg was on the ground with her left hand resting on the floor. ... It was crossed across the breast. Her face was no more than 5 or 6 inches from the club wall. ... The wall was not even a foot away. there was no evidence of fighting. The blood was liquid and had travelled toward the kitchen at the back of the bar. The portion closest to her on the ground was somewhat congealed. It is difficult to say if there was any still flowing from the throat. Doctor. Blackwell was the first doctor to arrive. He arrived a few minutes after me, but I didn't have a timer with me. The Dr. Blackwell examined the body as well as the surrounding area. Dr. Phillips came ten minutes later. Inspector Pinhorn came in right to the scene after the arrival of Dr. Blackwell. When I blew my whistle, the other constables arrived and I was able to have the yard's entrance locked. This happened during the time the Dr. Blackwell was looking at the body. Prior to that, the doors were completely to the outside. Foots of those who died were extended up to the swing of the gate to ensure that the gate could be shut without causing any harm to the body."

The doctor. Blackwell, who examined the scene of the crime was asked about the manner in which Stride may be killed. He said, "I formed the opinion that the perpetrator probably got this silk wrapper, tightly and knotted and pulled the victim backwards which cut her throat the manner. The throat may have been cut when she fell, or while she was lying sitting on the ground. The blood may have flowed around, if the crime occurred when she was standing up."

The jury also inquired during the inquiry how the length of time he believed Stride was dead when he reached the scene. He stunned his listeners by saying "From 20 minutes to an hour" when I arrived. The clothes were not soaked due to rain. She may have died relatively slowly due to the vessels on the one side of her neck being cut, and the artery being not totally cut off." This crucial information suggested that someone might be stumbling across the scene as the murder was taking place, thus not giving the Ripper to complete his task in the same manner the way he had done when he was with Annie Chapman or Nicholls. It was again up upon it to Dr. Phillips to perform the autopsy. The doctor reported "Over all shoulders and particularly the right shoulder, starting from the front, beneath the collar bones, and behind the chest, there is a blueish discoloration that I have observed and observed on two occasions since. From the left side of the neck to right, is an uncut incision of that is six inches long. the cut is 2 1/2 inches straight beneath the jaw's angle. Three quarters of an inch of the muscle that is undivided, and then getting deeper, around one inch, dividing the sheath from vessels, rising to a certain extent, before cutting into the muscle beyond and exposing the cartilages to the right side of the neck. The carotid artery that runs on the left side as well as the other vessels in the sheath were cut out, except for the posterior part of the carotid, which was cut to an area of 1/12th of an inch in length that prevented the segregation between the lower and the upper part of the carotid artery. The cut made through the tissue located on the opposite side is less pronounced and extends to just two inches below jaw's right angle. It is clear that the hemorrhage that caused death was caused by partial dissection from the carotid artery in the left. There is a defect in part of the bone of right leg's lower half that aren't straight, however, they bow forward. Additionally, there is a swell above the ankle of the left. The bones are straighter here. There is no recent injury externally, except to the neck. ... It was discovered inside the underskirt pocket of the deceased, a key like a padlock, an unimportant piece from lead pencil an unbroken piece of the comb, a spoon made of metal and two dozen large buttons, small buttons attached to a hook like it was a part of an outfit, a bit of muslin and two or three small fragments of newspaper. In examining her jacket, I discovered that, despite an eminent amount of mud on the right and the left, it was coated with the mud."

Phillips included other vital details in his thorough report:

"The body lay on the side that was closest to it, with the head turned towards the wall, the head towards to the yard and the feet facing the street. One arm of the left was extended , and there was a bag from cachous left in his left arm. ... The right hand was placed over the stomach; the hand's back and wrist was covered in blood clots. The legs were dragged up , with the feet pressed towards the wall. The face and body were warm, while the hands cold. The legs were warm.

"The deceased was wearing the silk handkerchief that was tied around her neck. It was a little damaged. I've now determined the cut. This was in line with it being the correct angle for jaw. The throat was swollen and gashed and there was a scuff of the skin that was 1 1/4 inches wide, which was stained by blood, beneath her right eyebrow.

"At 3.30 p.m. on a Monday, on Monday, at St. George's Mortuary, Dr. Blackwell and I performed an examination post-mortem. Rigor mortis was still well and clearly. There was some mud on the left of the face, and it was matted on the head. ... The body was quite well-nourished. Both shoulders, in particular the right side, and below the collarbone, and on top of the chest was a blue-ish discoloration that I've observed and witnessed twice afterward...

"Decomposition began to occur within the skin. Dark brown spots appeared on the front of the left cheek. There was a defect in both the bones on right leg that was not straight, but was bent towards the front. There was no external injury other than the neck.

"The body was being cleaned deeper, and I was able to observe some healing sores. The left earlobe ears was torn like it came caused by the removal or wearing by an earring but it was fully healed. When the scalp was removed, there was no indication of bleeding or the extravasation of blood. ... The heart was tiny and the left ventricle was firmly contracted, while the right ventricle was slightly contracted. There no clots in the pulmonary artery. However, the ventricle on right was stuffed with dark clots. The left ventricle was tightly contracted , and appeared to be completely empty. The stomach was huge with the mucous membrane was only filled with fluid. It was a mixture of partially digested food that was presumably composed of potato, cheese, and farinaceous flour [flour, or milled grainsThe stomach was large and full of food. The teeth in the lower left jaw were missing."

The time was right after Stride's death that one the most thrilling evidences in the case was discovered. Thomas Coram, a coconut dealer, described the discovery of a possible murder weapon "On Monday, just after midnight, I left the house of a friend in Bath-gardens Brady-street. I followed Brady-street straight and then into Whitechapel-road in the direction of Aldgate. I started along the right-hand side of the Whitechapel-road, but then crossed over to the left. at the intersection with No. 253, I found a knife on the front doorstep. ... The knife was that would be used by bakers in the course of his work, having a flat top, not pointed like a butcher's knives would be. The blade, colored with blood-like stains It was about a feet long as well as an inch wide while the handle measured 6 inches long and was strongly riveted at three points. The handkerchief was wrapped around it's edge, with the handkerchief had been folded, and then wrapped around the blade. A policeman was coming toward me, I directed at the blade that I didn't touch."The officer in the case was Constable Joseph Drage, later testified, "On Monday morning at half-past 12 o'clock, I was on fixed-point duty in Whitechapel Road, opposite Brady-street and I saw the final witness reach down to retrieve something about 20 yards away from me. As I walked towards him the policeman beckoned me using his finger, and then said: 'Policeman, there's a knife on the ground. I then noticed a long-bladed blade lying in the front yard. I picked it up and saw it covered in blood. ... An old handkerchief, also stained with blood, was tucked around the handle, and tied with strings. ... Then I was able to pass the step one time and a quarter earlier. I'm not sure that it was there, but I don't believe the knife was in there at the time. A little over an hour ago, I was standing near the door, and I saw the landlord let out an individual. The knife was not present at the time. I gave the knife as well as the handkerchief to Phillips. Phillips on Monday afternoon."

After inspecting the blade, Phillips determined that it wasn't likely to be the weapon used in the murder: "The knife produced on the previous occasion was handed to me in a secure manner by a constable and after a thorough examination, I found it to be the same knife that is commonly found in a chandler's workshop and is referred to as "a slicing knife. It is covered in blood which is like the blood of an individual. It was recently cut and its edges have been rotated by rubbing it against the surface of a stone, such as an Kerbstone. It was evidently before the sharpness of a knife.

The Coroner: Could it be as knife that caused the injuries that were suffered by the deceased? A knife like this could have created the cut and injury to the neck, however it's not the type of weapon that I could have focused on as having caused the injuries that occurred in this instance If my view regarding the body's position the body is correct, then the knife would then become an unlikely instrument to have caused the injury. ... The way I see it, am of the opinion that this cut created from the left towards the side that was deceased and based on the location of the cut, it is not likely that long knives caused the injury to the neck. The knife was rounded towards the top, and was approximately an inch wide. The blade was larger at its base. ... This cut was caused by cutting an edge across the throat. A shorter knife, like the knife of a shoemaker that is well-ground, could do the same."

As time passed and one man after the other was initially believed to be the Ripper and then dismissed due to reasons of a different kind There appeared to be an end to the investigation following the night when both Stride as well as Eddowes were killed, in particular because Stride was discovered so quickly after her death. Dew later stated, "The Berners Street murder revealed a clue that at times gave hope to everyone. Our investigation revealed the fact that just only a few minutes, or at any the very shortest time prior to the time of her demise Elizabeth Stride, or 'Long Liz' in the eyes of her friends, had been with one of the men. This information was provided to us by an individual who ran an artisanal fruit shop located in Berners Street. The man claimed that during the wee

hours of Sunday morning, he offered the couple a few grapes. The true significance of the vendor's story lies on the basis that he said that he'd seen the woman's friend previously and was certain to be able to recognize him if he came across him once more. The story was, however, backed by an account of the man, which can be described as ambiguous. It could have been applicable to a multitude of people. Then , a dramatic confirmation of his account. In the small Berners Street court, quite close to where the body was discovered investigators who were searching every inch of the floor came across several stone and grapes. It was obvious that they were the remains of the grapes Long Liz's partner had bought at the local fruit store and that she was likely to have eaten them up until the point of her passing. The only other possibility - that seems unlikely was that, at the time of the night or early morning, Mrs. Stride had let go of one man, and sought the company of another."
This was a possible break that everyone was looking forward to and the police put all their energy into conducting an investigation but only to see their hopes dashed. Dew added, "And now comes what to any police officer working in the investigation was the most heartbreaking incident of the entire Ripper investigation. After a few days of the murder, the shopkeeper met the man with whom he had sold grapes walk by his shop. He knew this man was thought to be Jack the Ripper. Tragic of tragedies He

let the chance to catch him pass through. He did not even bother to pursue the suspect. He was not even in the mental capacity to relay the details at the constable closest to him. In his shop, as the man in question hopped on the tramcar, and then vanished. Another person was inside the shop. He told him about his suspicions , but the time was not yet. The owner of the shop later said that he was scared to go out of his business. The moment the shopkeeper's story came to the attention of police, hundreds of cops were notified of the latest smell. It was too to late. Jack the Ripper, if in fact he was indeed him had been a fugitive, was once again disappearing into the void."

The grapes weren't the only important piece of evidence that came to light after Stride's death. A worker known as William Marshall testified during the inquiry "I witnessed dead on Saturday last. On our road, just three doors away from my home approximately a quarter of a minute to twelve. She was walking on the sidewalk facing No. 58, which is between Fairclough-street and Boyd-street. She was talking to an individual. ... The man was standing in the middle of the street. there was no gas light close by. The closest was at the corner, which was about 20 feet away. I didn't see what the person's face was in the clear. He was dressed in a black cut-away jacket and dark pants. He appeared to be middle-aged. ... He was wearing] a round cap, which had an elongated top. It was similar to the cap that sailors wear. Around 5 feet. 6in. The guy was quite robust. ... I'd like to claim he was a businessman but did not do the hard work. ... It was clear that he appeared more like the appearance of a clerk. ... The man was wearing no items on his person that I'm aware of. ... They stood there for] several minutes, and the kiss was between them. I was able to hear him say, 'You wouldn't not say anything other than your prayers. He was a bit slack in his talking. ... Then I didn't hear them say anything else. After that, they left. I didn't listen to the woman speak when the man's comment, she laughed. They left towards the street toward Ellen-street. They didn't walk past the No. 40 (the club where Stride's body was buried). ... When I was at my door from half-past 11 to 12 it was not raining even a drop. The deceased wore an unassuming black cape. The couple was standing between my home and the bar for around 10 minutes. ... The man was gazing at the woman and he was wrapping his arms around her neck. There's a gas lamp on the corner of Boyd-street. It was not close at the time they passed me."

William Smith, of 452 H Division, also testified that he had seen Stride later in the night, with one of his friends: "He had a parcel wrapped in newspaper that was in his hands. The parcel was approximately 18in. long and measured 6in. to 8 inches. broad. He was around 5ft. 7in. He wore a dark-colored wool deerstalker's headband. His clothing was dark. The coat was a cutaway. ... The man was bald and had no whiskers. I didn't notice his features at all. I would declare that he was 28 years old. of age. He looked respectable however, I was unable to define what he was."

The only other evidence of the Stride case was one small, but tragically important small detail. Doctor. Blackwell said, "I would like to add that I took this cachous out of his hand on the right side of him, and it was almost open. The cachous was tucked within the middle of thumb and first finger and was concealed from the view. I was the one who spilled the contents when I took them out of the hand. I believe that the hand loosened when the woman began dying, suffered a fainting state because of bleeding." This is why the victim passed away by holding a tiny fresh mint of breath in her hand. maybe just about to pop it into her mouth upon the "date's" suggestion.

In the meantime, one of the people who searched in the vicinity for evidence in Eddowes murder discovered an object that is still controversial until today. It was around 3:00 a.m. the following night the constable Alfred Long found a piece of fabric badly stained by blood. the investigation further confirmed that it was that was cut from Eddowes' apron. On the chalkboard wall of the Goulston Street tenement in which it was discovered was the following sentence: "The Juwes are the men who will not be blamed for nothing." The superintendent Thomas Arnold was called to the scene and noticed the graffiti, however, he decided to ignore this piece of information, and ordered the graffiti to be removed off the wall. Unsurprisingly, a lot officers in his department disagreed with Arnold's decision not to ignore the graffiti. A few weeks later, Arnold reported what he saw and justified his decision telling the press, "I beg to report that on the 30th September, my attention was drawn to a piece of graffiti on the wall at the front door of a dwelling at No. 088 Goulston Street, Whitechapel which included the following words"The Juwes are the ones who won't be blamed for anything and were aware of the the aftermath of suspicion falling on an Jew known as 'John Pizer' known as "Leather Apron who was convicted of an act of murder on Hanbury Street a short time prior to that, a strong feeling was prevailing against Jews in general, and since the Building on which the text was discovered was within an area dominated by this sect I was worried that if the writing was placed there, it would have been an occasion for causing the ensuing riot. I thought it appropriate that it be removed, based on the situation situated in a way that it was likely to be rubbered by people who were passing through and from the Building."

On the 25th of October in 1895 On the 25th of October Robert Anderson wrote to Dr. Thomas Bond and asked him to utilize his expertise in human anatomy and the nature of man to provide him with an information about the type of person who would be able to commit these crime. Bond's profile is believed in the eyes of many as being the very first criminal offender's profile in the history of police. The report began with,

"I would like to announce that I've read all the notes from four of the Whitechapel Murders which include:
1. Buck's Row.
2. Hanbury Street.
3. Berner's Street.
4. Mitre Square.

I have also conducted an Post Mortem Examination of the disfigured remains of a woman discovered yesterday in a small space within Dorset Street -

Chapter 9: Largely Rewarding Rewards were Provided

"The inquests into the women were able to yield jurors who were interested in knowing why the police hadn't been able to do this, that or another, however I don't have any evidence of any of them ever making any effort to help. One juror at the inquest of Mrs. Nicholls made just such an angry scream. Why don't police offer the reward for the murderer?' he demanded. "If the Mrs. Nicholls had been a wealthy woman who lived within the West End of London they would have offered PS1000. However, she is a very poor woman and therefore they do not pay any attention. Women have souls as other women. I myself would give PS25 for anyone that is able to share anything that can assist. It's all nonsense and no-sense! The reality is this: the Home Office is very chary in offering reward programs, and with very valid reasons as well. Of course, police can't offer such a reward without the approval of the headquarters. Let me clarify that it wasn't an issue of money in any point. Public and police-a well-known phrase of the time-were working hard. Whatever amount of money was handed out, it would not have made any difference. The righteous don't need blood money. There'd be money sufficient for the individual who brought this monster to justice. The money would

have come in from both the wealthy and the poor and there was the joy of the masses. Unofficially, large rewards were given. Many bankers, including great ones, openly said that they were prepared to offer huge sums of sums of money to anyone who provided details that led to the arrest of the Ripper. Unfortunately, the time to redeem these promises never came up." Walter Dew Walter Dew
After the double murder, reward packages were offered by a variety of organizations for information that led to the Ripper's arrest. Posters were put up throughout the Whitechapel region proclaiming that "APPREHENSIONS SOUGHT.
The M O R D E R.
PS500 REWARD
CITY of LONDON.
At 1.45 a.m. at the time of Sunday September 30, September, last year, a female with a name that is not known was found murdered and brutally killed in Mitre-square in Aldgate in the city of Aldgate. City. An amount of PS500 is paid to the commissioner of the City of London Police, to anyone (other not who is a member of an Police Force in the United Kingdom) who provides any information that leads to the identification and conviction of the killer or the perpetrators.
Information to be handed an Inspector from the Detective Department, 26, Old Jewry, E.C."
Another one was announced two weeks after, with

more details and also included sketches of the possible suspect. According to the advertisement: "The woodcut drawings, which purport to be akin to the people that were last seen with the murdered women, and published within the "Daily Telegraph" were not authorized by Police. Here are the details of the people who were that were observed:

at 12.35 a.m. 30th September Elizabeth Stride, found murdered at 1 a.m. The same day in Berner-street. man, aged 28 tall, 5 feet. 8 inches. with dark complexion. small dark moustache, dress black coat with a diagonal and a hard felt hat with tie and collar; decent appearance. Carrying a package wrapped in newspaper.

at 12.45 a.m. 30th of June, identical woman, in Berner-street - a man aged about 30 5 feet. 5 inches. The complexion was fair hair small, dark brown moustache, full-face broad shoulders, dress black pants, dark jacket black cap with a the peak.

The time was 1.35 a.m. 30th September, Catherine Eddows in the Mitre-square, which led to the church-passage in Mitre-square, where she was discovered dead around 1.45 a.m. the at the same time a man aged 30 tall, 5 feet. 7 to 8 inches. Fair complexion moustache fair medium build; attire with a pepper and salt colour loose jacket, grey cap with peak of the same material with a reddish neckerchief tied in a knots; the appearance of a sailors.

Information that needs to be passed on through the

Metropolitan Police Office, Great Scotland-yard, London, S.W."

On the 16th of October the incident became a more gruesome twist after George Lusk, then president of the Whitechapel Vigilance Committee, opened his mailbox to discover the contents of kidneys of a person that was preserved in wine, as well as this note.

From hell.

Mr. Lusk,

Sor

I'll send you the half of the Kidne I got from one woman and then prasarved for the other piece that I cooked and ate was very tasty. I'll send you the bloody knife that was used to remove it in the event that you just want to wait an extra few minutes

The signature

I'm waiting for you to catch me when you can. Mishter Lusk"

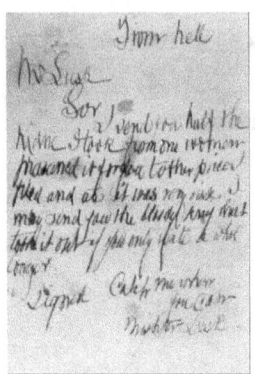

A photograph from the From Hell letter

Lusk

What is what makes this From Hell letter interesting is the fact that, while the inclusion in the letter of the renal organ (presumably Eddowes') would suggest that it is a good source for claims that it was he who killed the killer The penmanship of the letter was different from the penmanship seen at the bottom of the "Dear Boss" letter. Perhaps even more importantly it was clear that the From Hell letter was not made by Jack the Ripper. However modern examinations of the kidney included in the letter did not agree on whether the letter came from Eddowes and a number of investigators believed that the letter may be an act of prank played from a student of medicine having access to dead bodies' kidneys. However, the capacity modern researchers to compare the letters and study the kidney is limited by the fact that similar to similar to the Saucy Jack postcard, the From Hell letter eventually disappeared from the files of the police. The corpse of Mary Jane Kelly, the last of Ripper's "canonical" victims found on the night of November 9, and was mangled beyond comprehension. As with the other victims, her body was discovered in her own bedroom, lying in her bed. Caroline Maxewell was among the few who saw the deceased alive. She was later able to report "On Saturday morning it was 8 to half-past 8. I set the time to my husband's work being completed. As I left the hotel, she was in the opposite direction. ... It was an girl who had never been associated with one. I asked her across the streetand asked "What, Mary, brings you up so early?' She responded, 'Oh Carrie I feel awful.' ... She added "I've consumed a glass of booze and brought it up again' and she was on the middle of the road. I thought she was at the Britannia beer shop on the intersection of the road. I left herand said that I would be able to sympathize with her sentiments. I went to Bishopsgate Street to take my husband's breakfast."

Thomas Bowyer, who found the body in that horrible morning, recalled, "I went for rent that was due. When I knocked on the entrance, I received no response, so I tried again and again. In the absence of a response I went around the corner near the gutter spout. There is a window that has been broken - it's the smallest window. There was an open curtain. I put my hands into the broken pane, then lifted up the curtains. I observed two fleshy pieces sitting across the tables. The bed was in front of me near it. The second time I looked, I saw a person lying on the bed with blood and bloody stains on the floors. I immediately went quiet towards the Mr. McCarthy. Then we sat in the shop and I informed him of what I saw. The two of us then went together to the police station however, first, we went through the front window and McCarthy was able to look in to satisfy himself. We informed the police inspector at the police station about the things we'd seen. No one else was aware of the incident. The inspector returned along with us."

When the body was found It fell to the Inspector Frederick G. Abberline of Scotland Yard to investigate. He later testified "I received an alert of the Inspector Beck about the dogs that were being sent for, and the response was received to say that the dogs were in their route. The Dr. Phillips was unwilling to close the door because it would have been more beneficial to examine the dogs, in case they were indeed coming. We stayed there until 1.30 p.m. Then, Superintendent Arnold arrived, and advised me that the orders regarding the dogs had been rescinded and he issued instructions for the door to be forced. ... Then I later did an inventory of things in the room. There was evidence of a massive fire that had been kept afloat within the grate, to the point that it had burned the pot's spout off. Then we went through the ashes of the fireplace. There were fragments of clothing, pieces of the brim of the hat, as well as an untidy skirt. It seemed as if a huge number of women's clothes was burned. I'm sure it was to provide an illumination that would allow the person to check out the work he was performing. There was just one tiny flame in the space placed on top of a broken wine glass. The impression was spread across the globe that the killer took the key to the room. Barnett confirms to me that the key has been missing for some time and, since it's been stolen, they have placed their hands through the window that is broken, and then moved the catch back. It's quite simple. There was a clay pipe inside the room. Barnett said He smoked it." Barnett was Joseph Barnett who lived with the victim.

Frederick Abberline

Although a lot documentaries relating to the Ripper case have been lost, the report of Kelly's autopsy came to light in the latter part of the 1980s. It offers readers a horrific details about her demise. Doctor. Thomas Bond began with an account of the body at time of his arrival at the scene. He wrote "The body was naked on the mattress with the shoulders were flat, however the body's axis was tilted towards the left side and the mattress. The head was tilted to the left side of the cheek. It was placed close to the body, with the forearm being flexed at an angle of right angles and lying on the abdomen. Right arm disengaged from the body, and was resting on the mattress with the elbow bent, and the forearm in supine position with fingers locked. The legs were separated and the left thigh was in straight angles with the trunk and the right leg was at an obtuse angle to the pubic bones. The entire abdominal and legs was eliminated and the abdominal Cavity was empty out of the viscera. The breasts were removed and the arms were mangled through a number of jagged wounds, and the face was slashed to the point of no recognition of the features. The neck's tissues were cut all the way until the bone. Viscera were discovered in various areas, namely: the kidneys and the uterus, with one breast placed under the head, the second breast behind the foot that was on the right and the Liver behind the foot, the intestines on the right side and the spleen on one side. The flaps that were removed from the thighs and abdomen were placed on tables. The bed clothes in the right-hand corner is saturated with blood and beneath the bed was a bloody pool which was approximately 2 feet wide. The wall to the left end of bed at a point with the neck, was dotted with blood that had hit the wall in several different splashes."

Bond later went on to provide the details that he collected in the autopsy "The face was gashed all over the place, the cheeks, the eyebrows and ears having been removed. Lips were whitened and cut with a series of incisions that ran downwards obliquely to the chin. There were many cuts that ran irregularly across the entire face. It was cut in the neck through the skin and other tissues up to the vertebrae, the 5th and 6th of which were cut. The cuts to the skin in the neck's front revealed distinct ecchymosis. Air passages were cut in the lower portion of the larynx, through the cartilage of the cricoid. The breasts were both removed through small or circular cuts with the muscles running down to the ribs becoming connected with the breasts. The intercostals that connect the 4th, 5th, and 6th ribs was cut and the contents of the thorax were are visible through the incisions. The tissues and skin of the abdomen, from the costal arch up to the pubes were removed through 3 large flaps. Right thigh stripped ahead of the bone, and the skin flap, comprising the organs that are external to generation, and part of the left buttock. In the left leg, it was depleted of fascia, skin and muscles up to the knee. The left calf had a large gash in the tissues and skin, reaching that reached deep muscles and stretching from the knee up to five inches beyond the ankle. Both forearms and arms showed large and jagged cuts. The thumb on the right side was swollen by a superficial cut approximately 1 inch long with blood leaking out of the skin. There were numerous abrasions to the palm's back in addition to displaying the same problem. After opening the thorax, it was observed that right lung had been only attached by the old adhesions. The lower portion of the lung had been shattered and torn. It was healthy and was attached at the apex and there were adhesions along the side. Within the substances of the lung, there were numerous Nodules that were a result of the consolidation. The Pericardium was wide below and the Heart was not present. The abdominal cavity contained food that was partially digested from potatoes and fish. A similar foods were discovered in the remains of her stomach that was attached in the intestines."Dr. Phillips also looked at her body and wrote about what he found:

Chapter 10: There is no more clarity on the subject than 15 years ago

"Many different theories are proposed. I'm not going to discredit the most absurd of them all. I observed an incredible amount of uncanny things during the time of Ripper fear that it would fit with the entire story were the most unlikely scenario to be the right one. However, I can't not ask why so many people still to this day remain convinced that the killer could have been an aspiring doctor or medical student. I've never believed that. There are plenty of people other than doctors that are skilled using knives. Why not a butcher or an animal slaughterer, or the owner of an East End stall? The rudiments of surgical expertise were needed to create the mutilations I witnessed. ... It is no doubt of the truth that Jack the Ripper is dead. I often think about what kind of end he came to- whether it was peaceful or if it was a violent, raving madman that the man he was in the moments of bringing his victims. In my mind, I can't imagine an individual lying on a tranquil deathbed. A word more. I was awed by almost every aspect of my job as an officer in the police force. There were times when I was able to even find a hint of humor. There was no pleasure or humor in the role I played in one of the most famous crime drama ever made- the mysterious case of Jack the Ripper." Walter Dew. Walter Dew The murders were never solved as of the 20th century, novelists have been speculating about who the Ripper could be. The crime writer Patricia Cornwall has written of her belief it was perpetrated in the hands of Walter Sickert, a German painter well-known because of the creation of "portraits" of different Ripper connected scenes, however, even though Sickert was obsessed with the crime and even suggested that he lived in the same hotel that was once utilized by the Ripper however, there is no evidence that could link him to the murders.

There is speculation that the Ripper was actually a fugitive from London around the middle of the 19th century, and then moved to America in the meantime, where he continued to commit gruesome crimes. After the death of a female whose name was Carry Brown in the month of April 1891 and the New York Police Department received an unusual note that they dismissed as the job of an eccentric.

"Capt. Ryan,

You believe that Jack the Ripper' is in England But he's not. I am here and I am going to kill someone on Thursday . So be prepared with your guns, but I've got an instrument that has killed more than your guns. The next thing you'll hear is of a woman who has been killed.

Myself,

Jack the Ripper"

Another possibility that merits consideration is the possibility that Jack the Ripper was actually an actual Jill and this possibility was contemplated by a lot of people during the time of the murders such as Sir Arthur Conan Doyle, the famous author who invented Sherlock Holmes. Doyle thought that women could be trusted by women and be allowed to get closer to them even in a dark setting as a man could be. In the Williamsport Sunday Grit suggested that Jack the Ripper might not be a man in a piece about a different murder that occurred on the 22nd of February, 1891. "The renewed Ripper enthusiasm in London has brought about a great deal of turmoil within Scotland Yard. The slyness that this criminal has, as well as the speed with which he seems to defy the efforts of detectives, makes the entire metropolitan police force angry. The department's heads are not alone in their resentment. But, there is more to it they're not able to recruit enough men to guard Whitechapel and simultaneously keep enough officers at the docks as well as on the river's banks to guard non-union workers from the assaults that are continuously attacked by unionists. There is no doubt that police officers that the brutal murder of the victim in Whitechapel this week was the work that of the same monster that has now added ten horrific crimes on his list. The mystery surrounding who the killer is has been heightened by the latest incident. When the policeman discovered the victim beneath the railway arch , her eyes were still open and closing, her hands were twitching violently in pain as her blood still pumped huge jets of blood from her severed jugular.

The policeman who discovered the body was close to a hundred feet away from Jack the Ripper as she was cut in the throat of the victim however he did not hear the sound of footsteps or the slightest rumble of a fight."

Many people are now skeptical that Jack the Ripper was killed yet again following the murder of Kelly on November 18, 1888. which could be fatally damaging this article's attempt at linking the murder of 1891 with the Ripper The article continued to quote The Dr. Lawson Tait, who declared, "Nothing is more likely than the possibility that Jack Ripper is a real person." Ripper is a large strong woman working in the slaughterhouse the cleaning process, and then as well in cutting meat. Also, in a handful of cases, the women who were found dead were not necessarily dead. Their bodies were cold. The perpetrator was too far away. The fact that security forces were this close to the perpetrator proves in a stunning way that the perpetrator was female. Let me explain why. When they discovered an alleged murder, police immediately made a loop around the area. No one was arrested or more precisely, no person was detained. They didn't search for any woman. It is important to understand that the person who was responsible for the crime would be thoroughly splattered by the blood. It would be impossible to hack and slice a human body using the Ripper manner without getting blood all over the place. A person who is smeared himself cannot have been able to clear himself repeatedly. The situation would be simple for a woman. Imagine that the murder has been committed and the victim is in the water. All she needs to do is pull the skirt up to the waist, leaving behind her petticoat on, and then fold the shawl which is draped on her shoulders and is tied around her waist. She could then walk through the crowd without the lowest risk of being detected. When it comes to washing the bloody clothing what should an individual do? Immerse them in hot water. The blood coagulates, doesn't wash off and stain the clothing. What is the best place to obtain hot water? How can he dispose of the bloody liquid undetected? Women are always in the wash basin and would place the garments in the cold water and after a few rub and soap them, they would get untangled, almost without stain and not suspect."

One of the women that was considered as suspects was Mary Pearcey, who was found guilty in 1890 of killing her lover's wife and daughter. It is certain that she been motivated enough to commit the crime however, as has been the case repeatedly and again, there's no evidence that links Mary Pearcey to any of the crimes.

Mary Pearcey

The book that is written about Jack the Ripper would be complete without some kind of new theory as to who was the murderer. One theory that may be worthy of consideration may be the idea that Ripper was not a single person but a large, possibly medical students that merged into a kind of a sick secret society. Similar to how today's street gangs frequently require a murder as an initiation ritual and so, these guys could had been able to send one member of the group to Whitechapel to commit murder, and then, later, to try surgical techniques on a woman they believed by them as a lesser human. If this were the case, students who were not there would be able to act as discreet watchmen and also to shield each other from being taken prisoner. Maybe they thought of them as having done something beneficial by helping advance the field of medical research in the face of women that society viewed with disgust. It was only after the murderer who killed the last victim ripped into Mary Kelly with such fury that the group realized the error of their ways and broke up. Even if this admittedly nebulous theory is true however, the way in the manner in which serial killers committed the murders has convinced many that individuals and women across London and perhaps elsewhere in the world could have been treated in their illness through Jack the Ripper.

www.ingramcontent.com/pod-product-compliance
Lightning Source LLC
Chambersburg PA
CBHW050023130526
44590CB00042B/1824